REFUGEE WOMEN

WOMEN AND WORLD DEVELOPMENT SERIES

This series has been developed by the **Joint UN/NGO Group on Women and Development** and makes available the most recent information, debate and action being taken on world development issues, and the impact on women. Each volume is fully illustrated and attractively presented. Each outlines its particular subject, as well as including an introduction to resources and guidance on how to use the books in workshops and seminars. The aim of each title is to bring women's concerns more directly and effectively into the development process, and to achieve an improvement in women's status in our rapidly changing world.

The Group was established in 1980 to organise the production and distribution of Joint UN/NGO development education materials. It was the first time that United Nations agencies and non-governmental organisations had collaborated in this way, and the Group remains a unique example of cooperation between international and non-governmental institutions. Membership of the Group is open to all interested organisations.

SERIES TITLES – in order of scheduled publication

- **WOMEN AND THE WORLD ECONOMIC CRISIS** PREPARED BY JEANNE VICKERS

- **WOMEN AND DISABILITY** PREPARED BY ESTHER R. BOYLAN

- **WOMEN AND HEALTH** PREPARED BY PATRICIA SMYKE

- **WOMEN AND THE ENVIRONMENT** PREPARED BY ANNABEL RODDA

- **REFUGEE WOMEN** PREPARED BY SUSAN FORBES MARTIN

- **WOMEN AND LITERACY** PREPARED BY MARCELA BALLARA

- **WOMEN AND THE FAMILY** PREPARED BY HELEN O'CONNELL

- **WOMEN AT WORK** PREPARED BY CHRISTINE ELSTOB

- **WOMEN AND HUMAN RIGHTS** PREPARED BY KATARINA TOMASEVŠKI

- **WOMEN AS CONSUMERS**

For full details, as well as order forms, please write to:
ZED BOOKS LTD, 57 CALEDONIAN ROAD, LONDON N1 9BU, U.K. and 165 First Avenue, Atlantic Highlands, New Jersey 07716, U.S.A.

REFUGEE WOMEN

PREPARED BY SUSAN FORBES MARTIN

Zed Books Ltd · London & New Jersey

Refugee Women was first published by Zed Books Ltd,
57 Caledonian Road, London N1 9BU, United Kingdom and 165 First Avenue,
Atlantic Highlands, New Jersey 07716, United States of America, in 1992.

Cover and book design by Lee Robinson
Cover photo: D. A. Giulianotti
Typeset by Goodfellow & Egan, Cambridge
Printed and bound in the United Kingdom at The Bath Press, Avon

British Library Cataloguing in Publication Data

A catalogue record for this book is available from the British Library

ISBN 1 85649 000 9 hb
ISBN 1 85649 001 7 pb

Library of Congress Cataloging-in-Publication Data

A catalogue record for this book is available from the US Library of Congress

CONTENTS

ACKNOWLEDGEMENTS

This book has been prepared by Susan Forbes Martin, Senior Associate of the Refugee Policy Group, on behalf of the Joint UN/NGO Group on Women and Development and made possible through financial contributions from:

- Austcare
- The Danish Refugee Council
- The Norwegian Refugee Council
- The Pew Charitable Trusts

Technical advice and co-operation were contributed by the Office of the United Nations High Commissioner for Refugees (UNHCR).

The content of this book has been approved by the Joint UN/NGO Group on Women and Development. The following organizations have made a special contribution through their participation in the editorial panel formed for this publication:

- International Catholic Migration Committee
- International Council of Women
- International Labour Office (ILO)
- International Organization of Consumers Union
- League of Red Cross and Red Crescent Societies
- Lutheran World Federation
- Quaker United Nations Office
- Soroptimist International
- United Nations Development Programme (UNDP)
- Office of the United Nations High Commissioner for Refugees (UNHCR)
- United Nations Relief and Works Agency for Palestine Refugees in the Near East (UNRWA)
- World Council of Churches
- World Health Organisation (WHO)
- World University Service
- World Young Women's Christian Association

Overall co-ordination and management of the **Joint UN/NGO Group on Women and Development** is provided by the **United Nations Non-Governmental Liaison Service (NGLS)**, an inter-agency unit which fosters dialogue and co-operation between the UN system and the NGO community on development policy issues and North–South relations.

EXPLANATORY NOTE

THIS BOOK OUTLINES the situation of refugee and displaced women, discussing both their needs and the contributions that they can make and have made. It also describes steps that have been taken by the UN, governments and non-governmental organizations (NGOs) to respond more effectively to the presence of refugee women. Throughout, it makes recommendations for further action. As such, it is intended to encourage discussion and networking on what can be done to inform, organize and work to improve people's understanding of the situation of refugee and displaced women, and to develop programmes, campaigns and strategies which genuinely respond to the needs outlined.

The book can be used as a tool to help individuals and groups to stimulate reflective discussion and further research and study, and to encourage creative analysis with regard to possible solutions. It can serve as a basic guide to the subject; as a structure for study and a framework for subsequent action; as a basis for discussion groups and for conferences, workshops and seminars; and a means of informing and sensitizing voluntary organizations and government agencies. The audience intended for the book includes local and regional NGOs in both industralized and developing countries; women's and youth organizations, religious groups, development NGOs, trade unions and educational establishments; and agencies and programmes of the UN system.

Following a general introduction, the situation of refugee and displaced women and children is discussed in chapters touching on the following issues:

- the role of refugee and displaced women in their communities and their participation in decision-making and programming;
- physical and legal protection issues affecting refugee and displaced women;
- assistance issues, including access to food, shelter and water, health care, education and social services;
- the economic activities of refugee and displaced women;
- the search for durable solutions in developing countries, including repatriation and permanent settlement in countries of asylum;
- resettlement in industrialized countries; and
- the evolution of policy and programmatic actions at the international level to improve assistance and protection efforts for refugee women, including the staffing and training that can be undertaken to improve responses to the needs of refugee women.

Annexes include a development education agenda, providing suggestions for further study; the policy statement on refugee women recently adopted by the Executive Committee of the UNHCR as a model for other UN agencies, national governments and NGOs; other relevant UN documentation; and a resource guide, including a bibliography and a list of organizations working with refugees.

The contents of the book have been compiled from a variety of sources so as to provide a global perspective and a wide spectrum of views on the themes and issues concerned.

SUSAN FORBES MARTIN

PREFACE
BY SADAKO OGATA*

IT GIVES ME GREAT PLEASURE to introduce this book which represents the shared experiences of non-governmental organizations and the United Nations system in activities on behalf of refugee women.

In a constantly changing world, where political or ethnic strife can result overnight in thousands of people fleeing to preserve their basic rights, it is essential that we respond rapidly and efficiently to prevent potential tragedy on a massive scale. Yet it is also an essential part of these efforts that we occasionally take the time to reflect on our past with a view to improving our response in the future. I see this book as such an opportunity. I hope that in sharing our reflections with the general public, the reader will learn from our experience and be encouraged to work with us in supporting the efforts of refugee women in rebuilding their lives.

Even as we collected information for the book we became aware of gaps in our information. For example, relatively little had been documented on the specific issues facing women returning to their homes after years of exile. Yet we hope that 1992 will be the 'year of repatriation' for thousands of refugees who will now have the opportunity to return voluntarily to the country they may have left behind many years ago. Part of such an analysis is indeed discovering areas where we need more practically oriented research so that we can apply lessons learned by improving our delivery of programmes. I hope that

the information we have made available as well as the gaps we have identified will provide a challenge to academic and development organizations to pay greater attention to refugee situations generally and their impact on international development programmes.

I cannot underline enough the importance of the focus on refugee women. Although we try to ensure that our protection and assistance activities reach all refugees, we are aware that the specific situation of women may make them vulnerable to exploitation, and unable to benefit equitably from our efforts. We also know that many refugee families are headed by women, and that without specific efforts on their behalf they may become completely marginalized in their societies.

The cycle of hopelessness created by an impoverished mother raising a family on her own must be addressed as an issue of highest priority in refugee situations, if we are to create conditions favourable to future self reliance. Even in the first stages of an emergency, we are aware that the way in which we respond may set a pattern of encouraging refugees to participate in self-help activities or create potential dependency situations. This book provides practical and cost-effective ways to ensure refugee women's participation and it documents what happens if this critical element is forgotten.

We are committed to supporting the efforts of refugee women as partners in finding durable solutions to their situations. We hope that this book will make an important contribution to their efforts.

---

* UN High Commissioner for Refugees

INTRODUCTION
BY ANN BRAZEAU*

VIOLENCE, TENSION, TOTAL DISREGARD of human rights, poverty, and ecological degradation continue to feed refugee flows. The sudden uprooting of thousands of people has become a frequent and major focus of international humanitarian assistance in this decade. A significant number of these refugees are women and their dependants, many having lost husbands and fathers in the chaos of flight. It is, therefore, timely that a book is published which will help development and humanitarian assistance practitioners respond to the unique and complex challenges raised in delivering programmes effectively to refugees generally, and refugee women in particular.

There are over 20 million refugees in the world today, and 20 million displaced within the borders of their own countries. Most live in developing nations whose already fragile resources and infrastructure can barely sustain the needs of their own nationals. Many stay for prolonged periods in the country of first asylum before they can safely return home. Some may never return home and have little choice but to rebuild their lives in a new country. Regardless of the ultimate solution to a specific refugee movement, it is obvious that major development issues are raised by the process itself. Root causes of mass flight can be a complex mixture of social, economic, ethnic and political factors which must be analysed carefully and taken into consideration in long-term development planning for potential refugee-producing countries and their neighbours. Too often, refugee movements are seen as an unexpected emergency which requires a short-term relief response, rather than as a logical result of a sometimes predictable breakdown in the socioeconomic structure of the affected country requiring a sustained response linked to development initiatives. Refugee movements must be seen as a critical factor in mainstream development planning rather than as peripheral to it. In the same way, inclusion of refugee women in such planning must be perceived as essential to efficient delivery of these programmes.

Refugee women face particular hardships at all stages in flight, up to the eventual resolution of their situation. A knowledge of these factors will assist refugee workers in planning activities which may alleviate some of the difficulties. This book does not promote refugee women at the expense of other family members but points to their specific needs within the refugee community with a view to ensuring that they have as much opportunity to realize their hopes as do other sectors of the population. Women in Development experts have emphasized consistently the critical and often hidden role of the woman in developing-country economies and her more obvious role as household manager and primary care-giver. In the refugee setting she must assume these traditional responsibilities in new and unfamiliar surroundings. As well, in the absence of male family members, she may have to assume the tasks they have traditionally carried out. Often the traditional support systems have broken down and she may find herself solely responsible for the welfare of the family. She herself may be physically exhausted and traumatized from her flight, and other family members may be injured or ill and requiring special care. If the family is to survive and begin to prepare for a self-reliant future it is obvious that assistance activities must be targeted to this most stressed proportion of the population.

A particular concern for a refugee woman is her own physical protection and that of her family. When she leaves her country, she can no longer benefit from the legal systems intended to protect her. This book addresses particularly those protection problems unique to women. Often she finds herself in potentially exploitative situations, entirely dependent on others for the basic necessities of life. Well-planned assistance activities recognize the importance of building in mechanisms which will limit this vulnerability.

A major theme of this book stresses the importance of refugee participation in the planning and implementation of programmes, as this is intrinsic to development planning yet is often forgotten in the rush and urgency of a relief response. When the immediate emergency is over refugees can too easily become passive beneficiaries of aid, rather than active participants in a dynamic process of developing self-reliance. It is refugee women who often bear the brunt of emergency planning oriented solely towards logistical operations at the expense of people-focused needs and resources assessment. Too often they are victims of distribution systems which do not take traditional socio-cultural roles into consideration, with the result that the most vulnerable groups are unable to have access to even basic rations. Ways of avoiding this unintentional bias and ensuring that women benefit equitably from activities are suggested.

For refugee women all three of the traditional 'durable solutions' – voluntary return home, integration in the country of asylum, and resettlement in a third country – pose unique problems. These can be related to re-adapting to traditional roles after having been forced by circumstances as a refugee to assume new responsibilities, or to adapting to new roles imposed by settlement in Western industrialized countries while at the same time conforming to her family's traditional expectations. Refugee workers assisting in the process of repatriation, integration, and resettlement will find chapters 5 and 6 particularly helpful in providing guidance in planning responses to these problems.

All refugees bring with them unique skills and resources. It is the aim of this book to share the concerns of refugee women so that we can assist them by providing them with every opportunity to realize their full potential.

---

* Senior Co-ordinator for Refugee Women at UNHCR

Ethiopian woman with a ration card.

SETTING THE SCENE

We enter the refugee camp through a military guardpost. We see rows upon rows of huts, stretching back into the camp for what must be miles. Ringing the huts are larger buildings, housing an infirmary, administration building, rudimentary hospital, training facility and food warehouse. Off to one side is a school.

Out of the jeep and wandering on foot, our senses are assailed. The smells of cooking food mingle with the stench of latrines. Dress ranges from the most traditional to the most modern, running shoes vying with native costume. Little stalls sell spices, salt, cigarettes, and candy for the children.

One impression stands out above all others, though: the faces of the refugees are overwhelmingly the faces of women and children. For these women, life is hard and often dangerous. They are the victims of war and repression. Many barely survived their flight from Cambodia. Some have been displaced for a decade, watching as children are born far from their homes and grow up amid barbed wire.[1]

MORE THAN 20 million people are refugees, having been uprooted from their homes and forced to seek safety in other countries. They are the victims of persecution, human rights abuses, conflicts and civil strife. An even larger number of people is displaced within their own countries for reasons similar to those causing refugee movements. About 80 per cent of these uprooted people are women and children, many of whom live in women-headed households.

The term refugee has been defined by the UN Convention Relating to the Status of Refugees as a person who:

owing to well-founded fear of being persecuted for reasons of race, religion, nationality, membership of a particular social group or political opinion is outside the country of his nationality and is unable or, owing to such fear, is unwilling to avail himself of the protection of that country; or who, not having a nationality and being outside the country of his former habitual residence as a result of such events, is unable or, owing to such fear, is unwilling to return to it.

The definition has been extended in Africa, through a Convention approved by the Organization of African Unity (OAU), to cover any person who 'owing to external aggression, occupation, foreign domination or events seriously disturbing public order in either part of or the whole country, is compelled to seek refuge outside his country of origin'.

Because refugee status inherently implies movements across international borders, a joint responsibility between international organizations and national governments has existed for some time and has been codified in international law. Primary responsibility for refugee protection and assistance rests with the UN High Commissioner for Refugees (UNHCR). In addition, the UN Relief and Works Agency for Palestine Refugees in the Near East (UNRWA) provides education, health relief and social services to Palestine refugees in Lebanon, Syria, Jordan, the West Bank and Gaza Strip, and the UN Border Relief Operation (UNBRO) has responsibility for providing assistance to Cambodians displaced along the Thai–Cambodian border. Other UN agencies, such as the World Food Programme

1

Table 1.1: REFUGEES AND ASYLUM SEEKERS IN NEED OF PROTECTION AND/OR ASSISTANCE
(as of 31 December, 1990, by region/country)

Refugees and asylum seekers who require international protection and/or assistance are unable or unwilling to repatriate due to fear of persecution and violence in their homelands. Table 1.1 does not include refugees permanently settled in other countries. In some cases, refugees listed in Table 1.1 may no longer require assistance, but still need international protection. Starting in 1989 USCR began to include asylum seekers in Table 1.1 recognizing the increasing numbers of countries worldwide that have instituted asylum adjudication procedures and the need for protection and assistance while their claims are pending. In this Table, the totals for asylum seekers (primarily in Europe and North America) are for those persons who applied for asylum during the past year. Hundreds of thousands of other cases are pending from previous years.

Asylum country	Total	Asylum country	Total	Asylum country	Total
Africa		**East Asia and the Pacific**		**Latin America and the Caribbean**	
Algeria	189,400 *	China	5,000	Argentina	1,800
Angola	11,900	Hong Kong	52,000	Belize	6,200
Benin	800	Indonesia	20,500	Bolivia	100
Botswana	1,000	Japan	800	Brazil	200
Burkina Faso	300	Korea	200	Colombia	700
Burundi	90,700 *	Macau	200	Costa Rica	26,900
Cameroon	6,900	Malaysia	14,600	Cuba	3,000
Central African Republic	6,300	Papua New Guinea	8,000	Ecuador	3,750 *
Congo	3,400	Philippines	19,600	El Salvador	600
Cote d'Ivoire	270,500 [1]	Singapore	150	French Guiana	10,000
Djibouti	67,400	Taiwan	150	Guatemala	6,700
Egypt	37,800 [2]	Thailand	454,200	Honduras	2,700
Ethiopia	783,000 [3]	Vietnam	16,700	Mexico	53,000
Gabon	800	**Total**	**592,100**	Nicaragua	500
Gambia	800			Panama	1,200
Ghana	8,000			Peru	600
Guinea Bissau	1,600	**Europe and North America**		Uruguay	100
Guinea	325,000	Austria	22,800	Venezuela	900
Kenya	12,300 [4]	Belgium	13,000	**Total**	**118,950**
Lesotho	1,000 *	Canada	36,600		
Malawi	909,000	Czechoslovakia	1,600		
Mali	10,600	Denmark	5,500		
Mauritania	22,000 *	Finland	2,700	**Middle East and South Asia**	
Morocco	800	France	56,000	Bahrain	7,500 [2]
Mozambique	700	Germany	193,100	Gaza Strip	496,300
Namibia	25,000 *	Greece	6,200	India	415,800 *
Niger	800	Hungary	18,300	Iran	2,860,000 *[8,2]
Nigeria	5,300	Italy	4,800	Iraq	60,000
Rwanda	21,500 *	Netherlands	21,200	Jordan	929,100
Senegal	55,300	Norway	3,900	Lebanon	306,400
Sierra Leone	125,000	Portugal	100	Nepal	14,000
Somalia	358,500 *	Spain	6,800	Oman	3,000 [2]
South Africa	201,000 *	Sweden	28,900	Pakistan	3,668,800
Sudan	726,500 *	Switzerland	37,000	Saudi Arabia	300,000 [2]
Swaziland	47,200 *	Turkey	178,000 *[7]	Syria	280,700
Tanzania	266,200	United Kingdom	25,000	United Arab Emirates	40,000 [2]
Tunisia	200	United States	73,600	West Bank	414,300
Uganda	156,000 *	Yugoslavia	2,500	Yemen	1,300
Zaire	370,900	**Total**	**736,600** [6]	**Total**	**9,797,208**
Zambia	133,950				
Zimbabwe	186,000 *				
Total	**5,441,350**			**Grand total**	**16,687,2009**

Notes

* Indicates sources vary significantly in the number reported.
1. By 31/3/91, there were 298,000 Liberians in Côte d'Ivoire.
2. Although Iraqi forces withdrew from Kuwait, and some Kuwaitis returned home, most who fled remained in countries of asylum as of 31/3/91.
3. By 1/5/91, there were approximately 600,000 Somalis in Ethiopia.
4. By 31/3/91, there were 23,100 Somalis and 6,000 Ethiopians in Kenya.
5. By 1/5/91, there were less than 35,000 Ethiopians remaining in Somalia.
6. Except for Turkey, numbers in Europe and North America represent persons who applied for asylum in 1990. The top four source countries for asylum seekers in Europe in 1990 were Romania, Turkey, Yugoslavia, and Lebanon. Hundreds of thousands of asylum applications from previous years remain backlogged in Europe and North America.
7. By 1/5/91, another 400,000 Iraqi refugees had entered Turkey or were living in Iraq in close proximity to the Turkish border.
8. By 1/5/91, another 1,300,000 Iraqi refugees had entered Iran.
9. By May 1991, as a result of the changes as in notes 1–8 above, the grand total had grown to 18,335,200.

Table 1.2: SELECTED LIST OF SIGNIFICANT POPULATIONS OF INTERNALLY DISPLACED CIVILIANS
(as of 31 December 1990)

Table 1.2 identifies selected countries in which substantial numbers of people have been displaced within their homelands as a result of human conflict, or as a result of forced relocations. Although they share many characteristics with refugees who cross international borders, they are generally not eligible for international refugee assistance. Because information on internal displacement is fragmentary, this table presents only reported estimates and no total is provided. It is important to note that even this selected list includes 20 million people, and that the total number of internally displaced civilians is undoubtedly much higher.

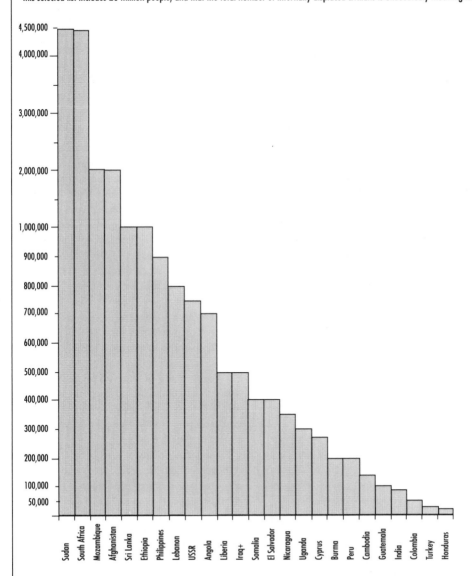

+ The number of displaced Iraqis increased considerably in 1991, to as many as two million people.
© United States Committee for Refugees

3

(WFP), the UN Children's Fund (UNICEF), the UN Development Programme (UNDP), the World Health Organisation (WHO), and the International Labour Organisation (ILO) are also called upon to provide expertise in matters related to their areas of interest. In addition, NGOs have traditionally played an important role as partners in the implementation of programmes for refugees.

Internally displaced persons are individuals who have left their homes because of persecution, civil war or strife, abuses of human rights and similar causes but have not crossed an international border. Overall, the responsibilities of the international community to such persons are not well defined, particularly with regards to their protection. The International Committee of the Red Cross (ICRC) has limited responsibility, its mandate extending to people internally displaced because of non-international armed conflict. UNDP resident representatives have responsibility for co-ordinating assistance to the internally displaced, but no UN agency has a protection mandate for those internally displaced that is comparable to UNHCR's mandate regarding refugees. Respect for national sovereignty tends to vie with humanitarian compassion when governments and international organizations are asked to intervene on behalf of individuals who are clearly still within their home countries.

Refugees and displaced persons are not just of concern to international organizations. They are and should be of concern to us all. Refugee situations, if left unresolved, can have serious consequences for:

- *The host country.* Most refugees have moved from one developing country to another, with a large proportion coming from and going to countries that are among the least developed in terms of per capita income. Often settling in the poorest areas of their host countries, the refugees can adversely affect local services, job markets, food costs, water supplies and the environment.

- *Regions in conflict.* Refugee situations can become explosive. The situation of Palestinian refugees, unresolved for more than 40 years, is a source of continuing disruption in the Middle East. The amelioration of most regional and internal conflicts in the world depends in part on a dignified and humane solution for refugees and displaced persons.

- *The world community.* Refugees are people with skills to offer and contributions to make. They contribute in countless ways to the communities in which they settle and are a resource for the reconstruction of their home countries. Yet, too often, refugees remain in temporary arrangements, dependent on international assistance, and their potential remains unrealized. Maintaining refugees in camps costs more than the US$750 million spent per year in contributions to international refugee organizations. Bilateral agencies, NGOs, and host governments spend untold millions more in the same effort.[2]

The greatest toll of unresolved refugee situations falls upon the refugees themselves, with women and children bearing the greatest costs, in the form of deprivation and unproductive lives.

Since the majority of the world's refugees are in the least developed countries, refugee women and children naturally experience the same problems as do other women and children in developing countries, that is, poverty, lack of adequate food and safe drinking water, large families, high rates of child mortality, and relatively poor health. But added to these problems are the special ones associated with the refugee situation, namely the

Table 1.3: MAJOR CONTRIBUTIONS TO UNHCR 1990

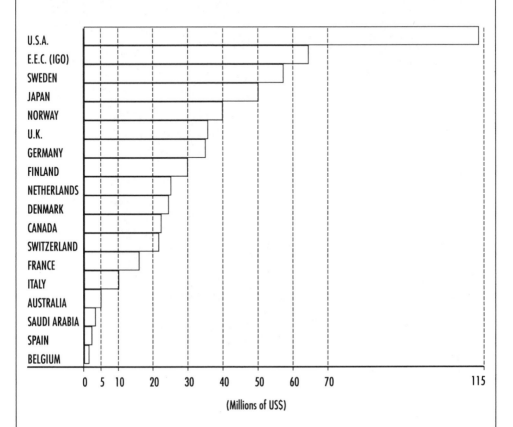

(Millions of US$)

Non-governmental Organizations and other Donors: 3,544,592

after-effects of violence, persecution, and other traumatic events. For all refugees and displaced persons, becoming uprooted causes major changes in their lives. The impact on women and children is particularly poignant and, in some cases, traumatic, particularly when rape and sexual abuse become commonplace. Yet refugees and displaced women are much more than problems to be addressed. They can make substantial contributions to the development of their communities if provided with the opportunities. At present, however, they are all too often an ignored, if not forgotten, resource.

The very fact that this book must begin with an estimate of the number of refugee and displaced women and children is testimony to continuing difficulty in effectively meeting the needs of this large population. That women and children constitute 80 per cent of the refugee population is a widely used statistic, yet its implications for programming and policy development have not been fully integrated into decision-making.

This is not to say that there has been no progress in improving responses. During the past decade, greater policy attention has been brought to the issues of refugee women within both the UN system and many NGOs. The UN High Commissioner

PHOTO: LEAGUE OF RED CROSS AND RED CRESCENT SOCIETIES

Palestinian woman with child.

for Refugees has now adopted a policy statement on refugee women, providing a framework for continuing improvements. The international NGO Working Group on Refugee Women, which organized an important conference in 1988, continues to focus attention on the work still to be done. In individual countries, organizations devoted to advocacy on behalf of refugee women have been established, helping to ensure that governments and the private sector do their share to respond to the women's needs.

Yet much remains to be done, particularly in implementing policy. Thorough assessments of the needs of refugee and displaced women in specific countries and camps have not been made, and, consequently, effective support programmes await design and implementation in most locations. Relative to men, refugee and displaced women still experience difficulties in gaining access to important services, such as income-generating projects and education programmes.

Perhaps most important, the significant contributions that refugee and displaced women can bring to bear in asylum situations have not been fully utilized. Without greater attention both to their needs and potential contributions, finding durable solutions to what in many places have become seemingly intractable refugee situations will be still more difficult.

1   Author's journal, visit to Site II, Thailand, November
    1986

2   Adapted from Refugee Policy Group, n.d.

2 CHANGING ROLES

Things are no longer as they used to be! You have to face up to things and adjust to the situation. We are refugees.[1]

For most refugee and displaced women, the refugee experience requires continuing response to change, including the need to cope with traumatic new circumstances. Forced to leave their homes because of persecution and violence, the women must often cope with new environments, new languages, new social and economic roles, new community structures, new familial relationships, and new problems. At the same time, they seek generally to reconstruct familiar lifestyles as much as is physically and socially possible. In a sense then, such women are both agents of change and sources of continuity and tradition.

DISPLACEMENT □ Family and community structures are profoundly affected by displacement, particularly when movements are involuntary responses to violence and abuses. Refugees move not because they wish to make better lives for themselves in other places but because they are forced to leave in order to seek safety. The decision to move is often sudden, occurring when families have exhausted all other remedies. Often, it is the disintegration of longstanding family and community resources that triggers the actual decision to flee. The refugees realize that there is little to keep them in their home villages or towns because everything of importance has already been destroyed.

Upon becoming refugees, families must deal with many new living arrangements. Families lose one or more members. Fathers have died in fighting or have joined government or rebel military forces, leaving women as heads of households. Younger children and older relatives have died of hunger or disease along the route to refuge. Others die soon after entering a refugee camp, too malnourished to survive even after help is offered. Still more family members succumb to epidemics that overcome crowded encampments in the first weeks and months of the crisis. Families are separated during flight, ending up in different camps or even different countries of asylum. Traditional family patterns are thus disrupted, leaving refugees with neither intact nuclear families nor extended ones.

Once in camp, refugees often find themselves living with strangers. Used to small, stable villages, they must now cope with large encampments, sometimes with residents numbering in the tens or even hundreds of thousands. Members of different tribes and clans are expected to live side by side, even if they were traditional enemies. The layout of the encampments will often differ dramatically from the traditional village pattern. People are assigned to specific sites on a first-come, first-served basis. In other situations, refugees and displaced persons from rural areas move to urban centres in either a host country or their own. They often do not know if their stay will be short, with return to their homes possible, or extended, stretching into decades or even longer.

Some are transported thousands of miles away to resettlement countries with completely new cultures and languages. Others, themselves, choose to seek asylum in Europe or North America. For those among these refugees who come from developing countries, uprootedness means adapting to industrialized societies and the changes in economic and social systems that development brings.

For refugee women, these changes in

family and community structures hold many ramifications. Uprootedness does not mean the same to all refugees:

According to the depth of the gap differentiating the roles of women in the refugees' society of origin and in their country of resettlement, refugee women may see a fundamental continuity between their experiences as women at home and those of the women native to their new communities, may come to question their own accustomed position in society as a result of having confronted alternative social patterns, or may experience a sense of loss as a result of the greatly different reality they now face.[2]

Yet, some issues appear to be common to most refugee and displaced women regardless of their location, even if they play out differently in different geographic contexts:

- The women remain responsible for most domestic activities, whether in Third World camps or industrialized countries. It has been pointed out in studies in several camps that women's day-to-day role often changes little, while the same cannot be said for their husbands who no longer are able to cultivate fields or engage in outside employment. The frustrations experienced by the men can result in increased family tension and potential for violence. The domestic activities of women are time-consuming and, in the refugee context, potentially dangerous. For example, women usually collect water and firewood, both of which may sometimes be found in mine-infested areas.

- Refugee women worldwide must cope with changes in family structures and roles. As noted above, the women often find themselves as heads of households,

Ethiopian women carrying firewood.

PHOTO: UNHCR/L. GUBB

with no husband or older children to help support the families. In such cases, women must either accept external help, generally through formal international or national assistance systems, or take on new economic roles to support their families by themselves.

In intact families, women must deal with the changes in female/male roles. Women in camps continue to be productive members of the family, but men often find they are unable to fulfil their traditional productive roles. In industrialized societies, refugee families soon discover that they are unable to become self-supporting with only one person's wages. Women may enter the outside labour market in order to help the family gain financial independence. Refugee men may have a difficult time in accepting either the new role of women or their own inability fully to support their families. This loss of control may result in domestic violence, depression and/or alcoholism.

Parent/child relationships also change as a result of uprooting. Younger members of the family are often able to adjust more quickly to the demands of the new situation. In both camps and industrialized societies, the younger people more easily pick up new languages, either the languages spoken by expatriates in the camps or the language of the new resettlement country. As a result children, including older girls, are often able to assume economic roles that are unavailable to their parents. They also become the conduit for information and translators for their parents. In a sense, then, the children may take on the typical role of the parent, being the force for socializing their elders to a new culture.

Intergenerational tensions often result

from these changes in role. A Vietnamese refugee mother in France who spoke little French stated of her children: They are ashamed of me, whereas at home nobody is ashamed of a member of the family, even one who is handicapped.[3]

- Refugee women often experience a new role as principal maintainers of the traditional culture. The custom of purdah is illustrative. It is perhaps the most striking attempt in a refugee situation to preserve what are seen as traditional values through the imposition of a specific role on women. Purdah is the Islamic practice that requires women to be secluded and kept separate from men to whom they are unrelated. In Afghan refugee camps in Pakistan, the use of purdah has been intensified and affects both rural and urban Afghan women who rarely had to practise it in their own homeland. In part, purdah is the result of the changed living situation in Pakistan. Women who lived among extended family members in rural Afghanistan were under fewer social restrictions than are women in the refugee villages today, because the latter are in closer proximity to large numbers of non-family members.

The intensification also reflects the fundamentalist strain in the Afghan resistance which opposes liberalization of the role of women under the current government in Afghanistan. Requiring strict observance of traditional practices among Afghan women has become a symbol of the jihad, or holy war. As a graphic example of this situation, programmes designed for refugee women were attacked in 1990, and staff working in these programmes were threatened. The exact source of the attacks is unknown, but it is widely believed that Afghan fundamentalists were responsible. The reverberations of this violence could be felt beyond the existing programmes. An international organization had to cancel a planned mission to the refugee camps later in the year because of security concerns. The mission was to have looked at the situation facing disabled Afghan women.

Often, this role as 'preservers of the culture' creates intergenerational conflicts for women. In many situations, older refugees are expected to be the preservers of the traditional culture while the younger generation copes with the new life. Sometimes this division of responsibility can lead to tensions between older and younger women, particularly when younger women are unwilling to assume the traditional roles:

Relations between older and younger generations of women may be especially affected by the refugee experience because of differences in the way each perceives the need to change or to maintain traditional ways of life. In Nasir Bagh [the camp for Afghan widows in Pakistan] new conflicts between groups have arisen. Many of the younger women, enjoying a first taste of freedom, want to go further in defying tradition. They speak, for example, of the possibility of remaining single after having been widowed, rather than marrying the brothers of their late husbands as is customary. Older women, on the other hand, see themselves, especially in the absence of men, as responsible for transmitting traditional practices to the younger generation, and view the younger women's rebellion against remarriage as a threat to the honorable fulfillment of their duty as Afghan, and Islamic, women.[4]

- When given the opportunity, refugee women form effective new social systems that provide support for their family members and the potential for helping others. Perhaps the most signifi-

cant thing that one can say about refugee women is that they are resilient and inventive. In the face of these various demanding changes and often limitations in their roles, examples abound of women forming new communities and support systems: an Afghan women's centre in Peshawar, women's farming co-operatives in Somalia, women's self-help groups in France, and women's mutual assistance associations in the United States. These women-initiated ventures bode well for the fuller participation of women in the lives of their new communities if the resources they have to offer are more effectively tapped.

P ARTICIPATION ☐ Popular participation has been defined in the development field as 'active and meaningful involvement of the masses of people at different levels (a) in the decision-making process for the determination of societal goals and the allocation of resources to achieve them and (b) in the voluntary execution of resulting programmes and projects'.[5]

While recognized as an important part of the development process, popular participation has lagged behind as an accepted part of refugee programming. As one commentator has noted, 'refugee participation probably has the worst ratio of rhetoric to reality of any concept in the refugee field'.[6]

Constraints on refugee participation include[7]:

- reluctance of host country governments to permit refugees a role in decision-making for fear of losing control and/or encouraging a sense of permanence among refugees involved in self-sufficiency efforts;

- reluctance of NGOs, particularly those involved in emergency operations, to establish refugee participation as a priority. NGOs often see community organization as an obstacle rather than support to their work;

- barriers deriving from the differences in culture and values among host country nationals, expatriate staff and the refugees themselves. These barriers include the more obvious language and cultural barriers that lead to misunderstandings and lack of communication, but also problems of racism, ethnocentrism and discrimination;

- conflicts within the refugee population. For example, conflicts between major ethnic groups or political factions can make refugee participation in decision-making very difficult when the refugees are unable to agree upon their representatives. Moreover, traditional leaders may be absent or find that their roles and capabilities are limited by the changed circumstances in a refugee camp or settlement;

- absence of qualified community organizers who can develop participatory programmes that are effective in a refugee setting.

Despite these barriers, the benefits of refugee participation are clear:

- It enhances normal coping processes; it builds self-esteem, rebuilds self-confidence, reduces feelings of isolation, and reduces lethargy, depression and despondency. Enhancing the capacity of refugees to cope with the after-effects of the refugee-producing experience is an important part of the search for permanent solutions.

- It is cost effective. Refugee participation can avoid many expensive mistakes. If refugees help with programme design, the programmes will usually be more effective than if they were designed by persons unfamiliar with the society and customs.

- It leads to self-sufficiency. Maximizing refugee self-sufficiency is a key goal in most refugee-assistance settings. To hasten this process, refugees need to be involved in planning and decision-

Afghan women sitting.

PHOTO: UNHCR/A. DIAMOND

making as soon as possible so as to avoid creation of dependency.

- It promotes protection. Internal protection problems are due usually as much to people's feelings of isolation, frustration and lack of belonging to a structured society as they are to any other form of social problem. Refugee participation helps build the values and sense of community that reduce protection problems.

Even within a weak system, the absence of effective participation by refugee women stands out. The situation described in Mexico in 1987 is not untypical:

Women's participation is limited in all the groups [the major organizational structure in the camps] and especially so in those groups comprised predominantly of Indians. In a number of group meetings that we observed, we noted that women were present but were unable to speak Spanish (the common language in which meetings are conducted), and participated little. For their understanding of the subjects being debated, these women were dependent on the occasional and partial translations given to them...

In interviews, both men and women noted that language ability constituted the major impediment to womens' participation. Nevertheless, upon closer observation, we concluded that language is not the principal obstacle. It is rather the shared view of men and women that women belong in the private sphere. The tradition in most Guatemalan families, and particularly in Indian families, is that womens' views are aired in family circles, and within this context, have considerable weight.⁸

Relief officials often point to cultural constraints in involving women in decision-making, particularly when their role in the country of origin has been limited. Looking to women as decision-makers under this circumstance, they argue, amounts to tampering with the group's culture.

Yet women refugees prior to flight typically had opportunities to express their concerns and desires through their husbands and traditional support networks, as noted in the Guatemalan case study quoted above. Refugee women cite their role in familial decision-making. A Vietnamese poem expressed the women's voices:

**We are the noi-tuong [home ministers] of our families.
For centuries our women have participated in the decisions that influence all that is important to us as families and as a society.⁹**

In refugee and displaced persons' camps, however, many women are unable to participate through such mechanisms. Not only are their voices unheard unless alternative arrangements are made, but perspectives they have to offer cannot otherwise be factored into decision-making. As will be discussed in subsequent chapters, in the absence of adequate female representation in decisions about such issues as food allocation, there will continue to be inequity in distribution systems as well as inefficiencies that could have been overcome.

While there is much to be said for maintaining cultural values, replicating traditional decision-making structures in a refugee or displaced persons' situation may also be fraught with problems. In effect, the culture of the refugees and displaced persons has already been tampered with. Social structures which existed prior to flight often become fragmented or destroyed when people are displaced. Deaths of natural leaders, and family separations, contribute to strains on the social order. In these situations, it may be impossible to select leaders on the basis of previous decision-making models.

Moreover, refugees sometimes live in a

virtual time warp. The role of women in their own countries may be changing dramatically (or might have, had the events leading to the population uprooting not occurred), but the refugees remain isolated from these developments. Within Afghanistan, for example, women have had greater opportunity for education, employment and political participation during the past decade, while many of the refugee leaders have tried to impose significant constraints on the role of women in villages in Pakistan. To further complicate matters, Western agencies sometimes impose their concept of what traditional women's roles were or should be, even romanticizing the dependency of women.

The problems that refugee women face in effectively participating in programmes and decision-making are compounded by an absence of reliable data about the demographic composition of the refugee population. As stated above, it is estimated that 80 per cent of the world's refugees are women and their dependants but we have little concrete data about the situation, needs, or resources of the people behind that statistic. As in the other areas covered in this book, even less is known about the experiences of internally displaced women.

There are two principal problems with data: accuracy of the statistics and lack of disaggregation by gender and age. Several mechanisms are used to enumerate refugees and displaced persons. According to the UNHCR Handbook for Emergencies, the most practical time to register refugees is on arrival, in conjunction, for example, with health screening. Reception centres are common, which allow incoming refugees to be registered and then transferred to a more permanent site. Such a system provides the advantage of being able to not only count arrivals but to obtain specific information about their health status, demographics, nutritional

status, and so on. The registration can also be used to distribute ration cards to the newcomers. Mass registration efforts are not always warranted, however. Where there is a possibility for quick return to the home country, extended registration procedures may give an impression that it is expected that refugees will be staying for longer periods than are necessary. Where refugees do stay for a protracted period, it is necessary to update the registration figures to take into account subsequent arrivals, departures, and births and deaths, a process that can be time-consuming and costly.

Where registration has not been feasible, a census may be taken using a number of different techniques: for example, counting the number of dwellings, if necessary through the use of aerial photography, or enumerating heads of households. Random sampling of the camp population is sometimes done in order to establish the demographic breakdown of the inhabitants.

Census counts in refugee situations have been notoriously poor. Both overly high and overly low estimates of population can have adverse effects. In Somalia, for example, census counts for years overestimated the population, and food rations were geared to the inaccurate count. Donors, convinced that the estimates were too high, decreased their contributions, leading to a reduction in the number of calories given in each ration. The assumption was that all families had more ration cards than members, but this was not in fact the case. Those families with an accurate number of ration cards tended to suffer most from this attempt to deal with the problems in the statistics.[10]

The second problem is the lack of disaggregated data on women and children. Each year the UNHCR reports on its activities and proposed programme and budget. A profile of each country is presented with numbers of refugees reported. While accurate statistics for all refugees remain a problem as discussed above, the situation is particularly poor regarding gender and age distribution. Of the 47 countries reporting more than 10,000 refugees or asylum seekers, only 18 provided some demographic breakdown of the population. The formats used in these 18 country reports differed significantly, making it difficult to draw firm conclusions about the demographic profile even within these nations. Some reported the proportion of women and children, generally citing percentages of 75–80 per cent. Others reported a female/male division but did not indicate what proportion of either group was adults and what proportion children. In only a few cases were figures given for the proportion of the population who were adult women versus adult men or for adults separate from children.

Information about such characteristics of refugee and displaced women as their education, skills, family size and composition is generally unavailable. Yet, all these factors contribute to the capacity of the women to be resources for their own families and their communities.

Participation of refugee women in programme management has occurred in a number of locations. For example, in Mexico some of the constraints on the Guatemalan women, noted above, have been overcome through the emergence of a refugee women's organization, *Mama Maquin*, in September 1990. One of the organization's aims is to select local representatives in different camps who will consult on assistance needs and participation of women in projects. *Mama Maquin* works with an Inter-institutional Technical Committee for the Integral Development of Refugee Women composed of representatives of UNHCR, the Mexican government and NGOs. The first test of this working relationship was a survey of refugee women's conditions in Chiapas. *Mama Maquin* was responsible for carry-

ing out the survey at field level, while the technical committee was to analyse the findings and make recommendations about projects to be implemented by NGOs and *Mama Maquin*. Preliminary findings have shown the need for literacy training.[11]

In a settlement in Zaire, female co-ordinators have been elected by the camp population (all members, not only women). The female co-ordinators' role is twofold: 1) they participate in the distribution process within their residential areas; and 2) they are responsible for what are termed 'women's affairs', that is, ensuring that pregnant women receive prenatal care; encouraging vaccination of children; and providing basic health education. The female co-ordinator also attends meetings of the otherwise totally male leadership.[12]

The Khmer Women's Associations (KWA) in the camps along the Thai–Cambodian borders provide similar avenues for the women's input into decision-making and implementation. The leadership of the KWA (which is generally chosen from the political parties that administer the camps) participates in discussions about issues that pertain to the camps' women and children. The KWA employs social workers who identify problems and needs within the camps; trainers who teach literacy, and sewing/weaving classes, and teachers who run day-care centres for the children of women in training classes.[13]

In a settlement in Zambia, a development–planning management committee was established as the mechanism for refugee representation in decision-making. At the time of an assessment by an international team, the committee comprised 17 members. Fifteen were refugees, representing the three nationalities found in the settlement (Angolans, Zairians and Namibians). The group included two village chiefs who had the responsibility of informing the refugees of decisions but who had not previously been involved in the decision-making process itself. The remaining two seats were occupied by Zambian community development workers who are employed by the government. Representatives of the voluntary agency responsible for increasing community development in the settlement, a partnership between Oxfam (UK) and the British Volunteer Service Organization, served *ex officio* in the meetings of the committee but had no vote. The committee included a number of women representatives who served at all levels in the structure. Women serve as the co-treasurer of the committee and as heads of the education,

health, and social and home economics committees.

C ONCLUSION ☐ The participation of refugee women in decision-making and programme implementation is a necessary step to ensuring that they are effectively protected, obtain assistance on an equal footing with men, have the opportunity to lead productive, secure and dignified lives, and are enabled to provide assistance when needed to vulnerable groups. It is a theme that must run throughout all refugee programming if the needs of the refugee community are to be met and solutions found for uprooted and displaced people.

1   Annick Roulet-Billard, in *Refugees*, Vol. 70, 1989, p. 26.
2   Sharon Krummel (nd).
3   Ibid, p. 13.
4   Ibid, p. 8.
5   UN Department of Economic and Social Affairs, 1975, p. 4.
6   Lance Clark, 1987, p. 1.
7   Fred C. Cuny, 1987.
8   Patricia Weiss-Fagen and Arturo Caballero-Barron, 1987.
9   Joh Tenhula, 1991, p. 93.
10 Angela Berry, in Ninette Kelly (1989).
11 Reported by the UNHCR Field Office in Mexico (1991).
12 Lance Clark, 1987a, p. 13.
13 Josephine Reynell, 1989, p. 118–9 describes the welfare programmes run by the KWA.

3 A SAFE REFUGE

Pich Kola is 13 and from Indochina. She has been living in a refugee settlement for some three years. The camp is guarded but recently armed gangs from her country of origin have broken in to rob and terrorize the refugee population. Pich Kola's family hut is on the edge of the settlement so each night they move into the centre of the compound and sleep huddled together in the open. One night a gang entered the camp and went on a rampage which lasted for over five hours. Those refugees who could not pay the money demanded of them were simply killed by the attackers. Pich Kola hid in a fox hole. Her mother and sister were however not so fortunate: they were shot as they tried to flee.[1]

PROTECTION IS AT THE HEART of the responsibility that the international community bears towards refugees. Refugees as a group are doubly disadvantaged and thus vulnerable to actions that threaten their protection. First, refugees are victims or potential victims of human rights abuses, conflicts and other acts of aggression. Second, they are outside their own countries and unable or unwilling to avail themselves of the protection their own governments should provide.

The basic structures and legal instruments to ensure the protection of refugees were established 40 years ago. The Office of the UN High Commissioner for Refugees was set up as of 1 January 1951, and the UN Convention Relating to the Status of Refugees was adopted in July 1951. The essential purpose of the Convention was to provide a general definition of who was to be considered a refugee and to define her or his legal status. Paragraph 1 of the UNHCR's statute formally mandates the High Commissioner to provide international protection to refugees falling within her or his mandate, and to seek durable solutions to their problems.

Women share the protection problems experienced by all refugees and displaced persons. They need protection against forced return to their countries of origin; security against armed attacks and other forms of violence; protection from unjustified and unduly prolonged detention; a legal status that accords adequate social and economic rights; and access to such basic items as food, shelter and clothing.

In addition to these basic needs shared with all other refugees, refugee and displaced women and girls have particular needs that reflect their gender and age: they need protection against sexual and physical abuse and exploitation, and protection against sexual discrimination.

PHYSICAL SECURITY ☐ While refugee situations can present problems of safety to all refugees and displaced persons, women and their dependants are particularly vulnerable. Their physical security is at risk both during flight and after they have found refuge. Protection problems can also exist after refugee women find such durable solutions as repatriation or resettlement. (These latter issues are discussed in chapters 6 and 7.)

FLIGHT The decision to leave one's home country is a difficult one at best. Generally, a combination of factors finally leads to a determination that flight is the only possibility. Refugee women are not always part of that decision-making process, however. As one Afghan woman described: 'My husband came in and said, "We're leaving. Women, prepare our things. We are taking as little as possible. All the rest will be left behind..." Deaf to our protests, he had made up his mind.'[2]

For many refugees, the violent situations that cause them to flee their home countries are only the beginning of the trauma. The path to refuge may itself be strewn with dangers. During flight, refugee and displaced women and girls have been victimized by pirates, border guards, army and resistance units, male refugees, and others with whom they come in contact.

They had just arrived from a small village in Huehuetenango, famished and exhausted after three days' uninterrupted march across thick forests. They walked alone and avoided the roads and villages where the unidentified armed groups wearing battle dress could find them.[3]

Abduction and rape may be the consequence of seeking asylum for those lucky enough to survive the trip. Piracy attacks in South-East Asia have been of particular concern, and the severity of attacks has increased in recent years, frequently with women as the specific focus. One eye-witness described:

Two of the young and pretty girls were taken to the front of the boat and raped. Everyone heard everything, all of the screams. That is what I remember, the screams. After a while, the screams stopped, the crying stopped, and there was silence.

You know it was a nightmare and everyone was part of it. You could not close your eyes. You could not close your ears. I still see the faces and hear the cries.[4]

A similar experience occurred on a second boat:

While all the men were confined to the hold of the refugee boat... some, if not all of approximately 15–20 women and young girls who were kept in the cabin of the boat were raped. The youngest of these girls was around 12 years old. Soon afterwards, the pirates set the boat on fire with all the Vietnamese on board. In the ensuing panic, the Vietnamese grabbed buoys, cans and floats and plunged into the sea. The crews of the pirate boats then used sticks to prevent them from clinging to floating objects... Women and children were the first to perish.[5]

Others have reported boat people being forced to choose young girls to be offered to the pirates in exchange for the lives of the rest of the passengers.[6]

An anti-piracy campaign funded by the international community to the amount of US$2.4 million per year has led to the arrest and conviction of pirates in Thailand. This campaign involves co-operation between a number of Thai governmental entities, including the Navy, marine police, the harbour department and the public prosecutor's office, and includes air and sea patrols, arrests of suspected pirates, and other activities aimed at suppressing piracy. The percentage of boats attacked has decreased as a result of these efforts. In response to the increased enforcement measures, however, pirates have intensified their attacks, killing more people so as to leave no survivors who can testify against them.

While piracy in the South China Sea has received much attention, problems during flight exist in other locations as well. For example, a refugee woman interviewed in Djibouti reported:

At age 18, she arrived from the two-week trek through the Danakil desert, physically exhausted, badly dehydrated, and with blistering sores from exposure on her feet and body. But the most terrible part of her ordeal, she points out, was the three days she was held at the border jail and raped repeatedly.[7]

Vietnamese woman and a rice cup.

Women separated from husbands and brothers in the chaos of flight or widowed during war are especially susceptible to physical abuse and rape. Separation of families often happens during flight. It is sometimes not possible for all family members to leave a country together; even when they can, families may be separated en route. Some would-be refugees, for example, Central Americans seeking entry into the United States, use smugglers to help them cross borders. 'Coyotes', as smugglers of aliens into the United States are called, sometimes separate adults and children at the final entry point, in part to reduce the likelihood that all members of the group will be apprehended. In addition, the presence of children sometimes makes it less likely that the border patrol will stop a group because more time is needed to process these cases.

COUNTRIES OF ASYLUM Violence against women and children does not necessarily abate when refugee and displaced women reach an asylum country. There are little hard data to document the actual number or severity of attacks. It is unclear, for example, if the statistics on one African country are illustrative: 33 attacks were launched by irregular armed forces against 21 out of 26 existing refugee settlements in the southern part of the country; 25 refugees died, 100 were injured, 300–400 were abducted, and 150 refugee women were raped.[8]

Aycha is 19 and from the Horn of Africa. She arrived in her country of asylum after a two-week trek through the desert. Physically exhausted and suffering from blistering sores she was directed to a refugee settlement but her ordeal was not yet over. A policeman of the neighbouring town raped Aycha after having threatened to have her sent back to her country of origin if she did not comply. The act of rape was subsequently medically confirmed. Charges have been brought against the policeman and Aycha is receiving care and assistance.[9]

Perpetrators of such violence include not only military personnel from the host country and resistance forces but male refugees as well. The abuse may be as flagrant as outright rape and abduction or as subtle as an offer of protection, documents or assistance in exchange for sexual favours; unaccompanied women and children are particularly at risk.

Prosecuting those who attack or exploit women has proved to be difficult in many situations. The women are often reluctant to talk about the attacks and to go through the emotional and sometimes threatening process of identifying and testifying against the culprits. The perpetrators may be individuals in positions of authority, and those representing the interests of the women are unable or unwilling to bring them to account.

In many camps, the physical facilities increase the likelihood of protection problems: camps are often overcrowded; unrelated families may be required to share a communal living space. In effect, they are living among strangers, even persons who could be considered traditional enemies.

Detention centres in Hong Kong, for example, have barracks housing 250 or more people. In the barracks, rows of triple-decker platforms serve as living quarters. A family lives in an area that is about three square metres. In some cases, families have pieces of cloth to separate their area from that of their neighbours, in others even this minimal privacy is absent.

It takes seeing Whitehead and Sek Kong Detention Centres to realize that the warehousing of people belongs to a systematic process of dehumanization, breeding violence and fear. It takes talking to a young woman who tells how, at night, she was

19

Vietnamese boat people sleeping.

raped by three masked men, while holding her child in her arms, to understand how little chance these people have.[10]

The poor design of camps also contributes to protection problems for women. Communal latrines may be at some distance from the living quarters, thereby increasing the potential for attacks on women, especially at night. Most camps are poorly lit, if at all. Night patrols to ensure greater protection may be absent or infrequent.

Incarceration in closed detention facilities compounds these problems. Closed camps are used in a number of countries where all individuals who enter illegally are subject to detention regardless of age or sex or their application for refugee status. Such camps are often surrounded by barbed wire, giving the appearance and reality of prisons with prison-like disregard for individual freedoms. Inhuman surroundings can beget inhumane actions.

Traditional mechanisms for protection of the vulnerable may be lost when refugees are forced to live in such camp surroundings. In particular, the communal support systems for protection of widows, single women and unaccompanied minors are often no longer present.

Spouse and child abuse and abandonment are problems encountered by women and children in refugee and displaced persons situations. Heightened levels of domestic violence are not infrequent where refugees have lived for extended periods in the artificial environment of a refugee camp. There is evidence that psychological strains for husbands unable to assume normal cultural, social and economic roles can result in aggressive behaviour towards wives and children. The enforced idleness, boredom and despair that permeate many camps are natural breeding grounds for such violence.

Refugee camps in a number of locations house the civilian families of members of armed forces and frequently serve as rest and recuperation sites. The men often bring weapons with them into the camps. Proliferation of weapons can compound the protection problems facing refugee women. Along the Thai-Cambodian border, for example, grenades can be bought for U.S.$.50.[11]

Forced recruitment of women and children into the armed forces of resistance groups is a further problem in some countries. In some cases they are recruited as actual soldiers, in others, they are required to carry ammunition and other supplies. In still other situations, women and children are used to clear mines. For example, recruitment of Cambodian women and children by the Khmer Rouge has been reported in Thailand: 'The witness added that she had been threatened with... conscription or imprisonment after refusing repeated requests [to carry guns and supplies to the Cambodian interior]'[12]

Because refugees and displaced persons are often associated with one or both parties to a civil war, the pressure to provide assistance to the military can be very strong. Not all such recruitment is forced, however: in some cases, refugee women may be active and willing participants in their community's struggle. For example, Palestinian women have been active in the *intifada*, the uprising in the Israeli-occupied West Bank and Gaza Strip. One of the newly emerging leaders of the Palestinian women's movement said:

For the first time, we are seeing women participating in various ways in resisting occupation ... in ways that we thought were not possible before the uprising. Women are now very active in neighbourhood committees. Their experience and organizational skills are facilitating these committees' work in providing services to communities. But they now participate as leaders, and not only as service providers.[13]

A Palestinian newsletter further reported:

The theme underlying the portraits here is one of open defiance of the occupation on the one hand and active defence of community and individual life on the other. We see rural women, women living in refugee camps, and a middle-class woman from a town responding with a striking similarity, despite their different circumstances. Defiance of the occupation and defence of the community: the twin watchwords of women in the Occupied Territories.[14]

Maintaining funding for programmes to provide for greater security for women and children has been difficult at times. During periods of budget cuts, the funds needed to improve camp design may be seen as unnecessary expenditures. Programmes funded through special appeals may be unable to maintain a constant level of support. To the extent that the needs of women and children are inadequately integrated into the planning and implementation of mainstream policy, programmes to enhance their physical security will be put at risk.

The failure to address adequately refugee women's assistance needs, for example, has had serious repercussions regarding the sexual exploitation of refugee and displaced women. Such exploitation takes many forms. In Guinea and Côte d'Ivoire, unaccompanied women and female heads of households from Liberia have been integrated into the households of relatives or local residents who receive food rations to help support them. While the system appears to work well in most cases, concerns about sexual exploitation of the women have been reported, particularly where the refugee women are expected to take on conjugal roles in their new households. As a UNHCR report noted:

There is a special need to accelerate the provision of appropriate accommodation to refugee women to ensure their safety and well-being as well as to see that they are not forced into a relationship against their will merely for survival.[15]

In other countries, lack of assistance has forced some refugee women into prostitution. It is unaccompanied single women and girls as well as female heads of household, who are primarily involved in prostitution. Refugee women without proper documentation are particularly susceptible to such exploitation. The causes are generally complex, but key to the decision to become a prostitute is absence of adequate income. Until alternative income-generating opportunities are made available to these women, prostitution will probably remain a too-common occupation. This problem is compounded by minimal assistance programmes in many urban locations, particularly where refugees are residing illegally. The reliance on prostitution is particularly acute where men have left their families to fend for themselves. There may be inadequate community resources for helping deserted families and/or inadequate community support for curbing prostitution.

LEGAL PROCEDURES AND CRITERIA FOR THE DETERMINATION OF REFUGEE STATUS ☐ Whereas in many developing countries assistance and protection are afforded on a presumptive basis to everyone from a given country who has crossed the border, in most industrialized countries and an increasing number of developing ones (for example, those of South-East Asia) individuals must show that their circumstances accord with the definition of a refugee. Even in those countries which do provide blanket status to incoming refugees, it is necessary to register and receive documents from the authorities in order to obtain assistance. Refugee women find obstacles in both situations.

STEPS TO BE TAKEN TO IMPROVE THE PHYSICAL PROTECTION OF REFUGEE WOMEN

- place international staff in border areas which refugee women must cross in order to enter countries of asylum as well as in reception centres, refugee camps and settlements;

- improve the design of refugee and displaced persons camps to promote greater physical security. Special measures that should be implemented include security patrols; special accommodation, if needed, for single women, women heads of households and unaccompanied minors; improved lighting; and physical barriers to the access of armed persons to camps;

- provide gender-sensitive training for host country border guards, police, military units and others who come into contact with refugee and displaced persons;

- ensure greater participation of refugee and displaced women in decisions affecting their security. Among the issues requiring greater input from refugee and displaced women are mechanisms to improve the reporting of physical and sexual protection problems;

- employ female protection officers and social and community workers to identify and provide remedies for women and children who are the victims of physical violence and sexual abuse;

- ensure that refugee women are not forced to stay for protracted periods of time in closed refugee camps or detention centres where they are likely to be the victims of family and intra-communal violence;

- provide emergency resettlement to refugee women who may be particularly exposed to abuse;

- offer gender-sensitive counselling to refugee women who have been victims of abuse;

- establish effective mechanisms for law enforcement to ensure that abusers are identified and prosecuted for their offence;

- incorporate information on the situation, needs and rights of refugee women in all educational activities carried out in refugee programmes;

- address protection concerns particular to refugee women in all other sectors of refugee programmes, such as health and nutrition programmes.

OBTAINING REFUGEE STATUS Women face special difficulties in obtaining refugee status. Two issues arise here: the grounds upon which someone is granted refugee status; and the process of establishing these grounds.

The UN Convention Regarding the Status of Refugees defines a refugee as a person who has a well-founded fear of being persecuted for reasons of race, religion, nationality, membership of a particular social group, or of political tendency. The claim to refugee status by women fearing harsh or inhuman treatment because of having transgressed their society's laws or customs regarding the role of women presents difficulties under this definition. As a UNHCR legal adviser has noted, 'transgressing social mores is not reflected in the universal refugee definition'.

Yet, there are examples of violence against women who are accused of breaking social mores in a number of countries. Amnesty International reported the case of a woman flogged in the street because she was wearing lipstick beneath her veil. Examples of lapidation of women accused of adultery, and of killing girls who have lost their virginity, are also documented.[16]

Even more of a problem are situations in which women flee their country because of severe sexual discrimination either by official bodies or in local communities. Protection from sexual discrimination is a basic right and is enshrined in a number of international declarations and conventions. While the universal right to freedom from discrimination on grounds of sex is recognized, and discrimination can constitute persecution under certain circumstances, the dividing line between discrimination and persecution is not clear. Discrimination can take a number of forms. In some cases it is the fear of ostracism or retaliation that causes a woman to flee, not because of her own actions but due to having been the victim of a crime carrying a social stigma, such as rape.

Women who are the targets of military attacks may also find difficulty in showing that they are victims of persecution rather than random violence. Even victims of rape by military forces face difficulties in obtaining refugee status. Amnesty International reports the following case which highlights the problem:

Catalina Mejia...testified that during a search of her family's home by the military in 1983 a soldier ordered her outside at gunpoint, accused her and her family of being guerrillas (which they denied) and then raped her. During the next 18 months she was stopped twice at military checkpoints in other parts of El Salvador. At each checkpoint she was singled out by soldiers, who accused her of being a guerrilla... She fled to the US in 1985.

The immigration judge presiding at her deportation hearing denied Catalina Mejia's application for political asylum in August 1988... He concluded that Cataline Mejia had failed to establish 'that she fears for her life or freedom, if deported to El Salvador'. One of the reasons given by the judge for this decision was that the rape of Catalina Mejia by the soldier who accused her of being a guerrilla was not an act of persecution but 'was more because she was a female convenient to a brutal soldier acting only in his own self-interest'.[17]

Similarly, women victimized because of a male relative's political activities often have trouble demonstrating their claim to refugee status. Yet, in many conflicts,

attacks on women are a planned part of a terror campaign. As one Somali woman described the war in her country:

The war in Somalia is an anarchist war. It is a war on the women. Any woman between the ages of eighteen and forty is not safe from being forcibly removed to the army camps to be raped and violated. And that's only the beginning. If her husband finds out, he kills her for the shame of it all; if they know that he has found out, they kill him, too; if he goes into hiding instead, and she won't tell where he is, they kill her.

Similar stories have been told of the civil conflicts in Mozambique, Guatemala and Eritrea.[18]

The European Parliament determined in 1984 that women fearing cruel or inhuman treatment as a result of seeming to have transgressed social mores should be considered a 'social group' for purposes of determining their status. The Executive Committee of UNHCR has not adopted this position, however, leaving it to states, in the exercise of their sovereignty, to do so if they wish. In the Note on Refugee Women and International Protection submitted to the forty-first session of the Executive Committee in 1990, the High Commissioner urged governments to take this step, noting:

In light of the increasingly universal character of the United Nations Convention on the Elimination of All Forms of Descrimination Against Women, severe discrimination, in disregard of this Convention, may justify the granting of refugee status in line with the reasoning [of the European Parliament]. In order to facilitate the task of determining refugee claim of persons who are in such a situation, it is important that decision-makers involved in the refugee status

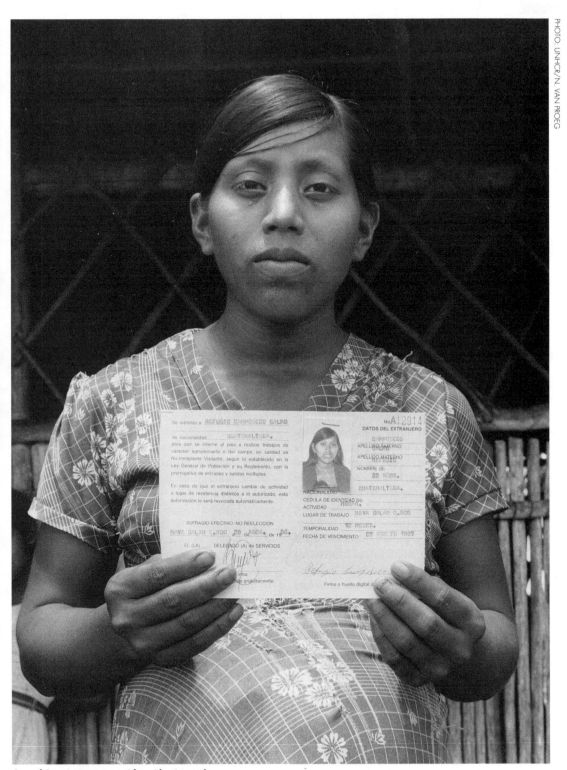

Central American woman with an identity card.

determination procedures have at their disposal background material and documentation describing the situation of women in countries of origin, particularly regarding gender-based persecution and its consequences.[19]

Even where the basis for persecution would clearly fall into one of the defined areas, for example, political opinion, women face special problems in making their case to the authorities, particularly when they have had experiences which are difficult and painful to describe.

Persecution of women often takes the form of sexual assault. According to one report on sexual torture, the methods of torture can consist of:

Either hetero- or homosexual rape; the rape of women by the use of specially trained dogs; the use of electric currents upon the sexual organs; mechanical stimulation of the erogenous zones; manual stimulation of the erogenous zones; the insertion of penis-shaped objects into the body-openings (these can be made of metal or other materials to which an electrical current is later connected, are often grotesquely large and cause subsequent physical damage, and are used on both male and female victims); the forced witnessing of 'unnatural' sexual relations; forced masturbation or to be masturbated by others; fellatio and oral coitus; and finally, the general atmosphere of sexual aggression which arises from being molested, from the nakedness, and from the lewd and lecherous remarks and threats of sexual aggression made to the prisoner and his or her family and threats of the loss of ability of reproduction and enjoyment in the future.[20]

The female victim of such sexual torture may be reluctant to speak about it, particularly to a male interviewer. Rape, even in the context of torture, is seen in some cultures as a failure on the part of the woman to preserve her virginity or marital dignity. She may be shunned by her family and isolated from other members of the com-munity. Discussing her experience becomes a further source of alienation.

The very delicate and personal issues arising from sexual abuse require the physical presence of officials who are trained and sensitive to the needs of refugee women. In most instances it requires female staff members who can talk with victims about their personal experiences. At present, women staff are under-represented in UN bodies and NGOs working with refugees, and too in many government bureaucracies that conduct interviews for determining refugee status.

Sometimes, women who arrive as part of a family unit are not even interviewed, or only cursorily, about their experiences, even when it is they rather than their husbands who have been the targets of the persecution. A wife may be interviewed primarily to corroborate the stories told by her husband; if she is unaware of the details of her husband's experiences (for example, the number of her husband's military unit), the entire testimony may be discounted as lacking in credibility. Yet, in many cultures, husbands share few details about military or political activities with their wives.

A further legal problem affecting refugee women is the actual status they are granted by a country of asylum. In most countries, family members who are accompanying or who join a person who is granted refugee status are granted the same status. This provision does not apply everywhere, however, nor is conferral of refugee status automatic for spouses and children who follow a refugee to a country of asylum. Family reunification is not a right conferred on refugees by the UN Convention; it is a recommended practice that leaves much to the discretion of individual states. While many allow family members to immigrate, a number of countries grant family members a residency status that provides less protection against deportation than does refugee status. Should the family break up, the wife (who is more often the person to be joining the one granted refugee status) may find herself without any protection against forced return.

Countries of asylum often have inadequate processes for registering and providing documentation even to those refugees who have permission to remain. Sometimes, they register and provide documentation to the male head of a refugee household but offer no proof of residency to other family members. Should the men abandon their families or be absent at any time, it is difficult if not impossible for their wives to prove that they are legally in the country.

Registration of marriages and births is a further problem. In some countries, no procedures exist for formally registering marriages and births that take place in refugee or displaced persons' camps. In other countries, registration can take place in camps but there are no procedures for the spontaneously settled. Alternatively, urban refugees can register their children but there are no procedures for those in rural settings. In still other cases, the procedures are in place but refugees and displaced persons are afraid to make use of them for fear of coming to the attention of the authorities.

Some countries of asylum do not even recognize as legal a marriage that takes place in a refugee camp:

After two years of camp life Pilar married a fellow refugee. Her marriage is however not recognized under the law of the country of asylum and there is no system of registration of marriages in the settlement where they live. The child born to Pilar last year is considered illegitimate.[21]

Statelessness is a problem facing many refugee children. In a number of situations, there are conflicting national laws concerning the attribution of nationality. A country of asylum may hold that a child born on its territory cannot have that country's nationality if the child's parents are of a different nationality. Conversely, the parents' country of origin, however, may hold that children are ineligible for its nationality if they were born in a different country.

Even where documentation can be legally obtained, constraints in registering exist for refugee women, particularly women heads of households. These constraints include physical and logistical difficulties in reaching the authorities responsible for registration, particularly in cultures that do not permit women to interact with strangers, and lack of access by single women and women heads of households to information about benefits to which they are entitled.

Failure to provide for registration creates many psychological and practical problems, particularly for refugee women who are the primary care-givers in their families. Registration is necessary not only to establish legal standing, age and nationality but also to obtain assistance in many locations.

The problems that can be encountered when refugee women do not have their own documentation were reported in a study prepared for the Economic Commission for Africa:

STEPS TO BE TAKEN TO IMPROVE LEGAL PROTECTION

- Reaffirm the political, economic, social, cultural and civil rights of refugee and displaced women, as stated in relevant international legal instruments, such as the Convention on the Elimination of all Forms of Discrimination against Women.

- Consider women fearing persecution or severe discrim-

---

ination on the basis of their gender to be a social group for the purposes of determining refugee status.

● Provide training to immigration officers doing status determinations regarding the interviewing and assessment of the claims of women.

● Employ women as interviewers and interpreters for purposes of determining refugee status.

● Use indirect questions to obtain indications about sex-directed persecution.

● Change procedures for registering refugees and displaced persons to ensure that women are provided appropriate documentation.

**During the late 1950s and early 1960s, many Rwandese refugees fled to Uganda en masse. In time, they integrated into the local population and became self-reliant, so that UNHCR assistance was gradually phased out. The recent disturbances, however, have uprooted many resettled refugees. Many have been widowed, and others separated or deserted. Thus, UNHCR has found it necessary to re-establish relief assistance services. In order to qualify for these services, however, refugees were required to present their identification cards, but most of the displaced women never had such cards.
A complicated and lengthy process resulted, whereby refugees had to prove their status which delayed access to urgently needed relief assistance. The problem of lack of documents is widespread and serious and requires an urgent solution.[22]**

INTERNALLY DISPLACED WOMEN ☐
Many of the protection problems experienced by refugee women are also felt by displaced women. Having moved from their homes for similar reasons, displaced women face sexual and physical attacks before, during and after flight. In one sense, however, displaced women are even more vulnerable than refugee women. Since internally displaced persons remain within their own national borders, it is often a government that has caused their

displacement that has primary responsibility for their protection.

Mary Awatch now lives in the third railway car from the front of the train. From the window of the same car, a year ago, she watched a man shoot and kill two of her children during the massacre at Dhein, in southern Sudan.... Mary and her remaining children are part of an estimated two million southern Sudanese who have fled their homes due to the civil war that is once again devastating the countryside.[23]

The institutional constraints on providing adequate protection to women and children in displaced persons' situations are substantial. No UN agency has a protection mandate regarding internally displaced persons although several have been involved in assistance activities for these individuals.

When these persons are displaced, however, either through armed conflict or internal strife, the International Committee of the Red Cross, according to its mandate as a specifically neutral and independent institution and intermediary, as recognized in international humanitarian law and in the Statutes of the International Committee of the Red Cross and Red Crescent Movement, endeavours to ensure them protection and assistance. In the case of armed conflict, persons displaced within their own countries are protected by fundamental guarantees relating to the treatment of persons who do not take part in hostilities under Article 3 common to the four Geneva Conventions of 1949 and by the Second Additional Protocol of 1977 which relates to the protection of victims of non-international armed conflicts.

Furthermore, women benefit from special protection. Article 4 of the Second Additional Protocol forbids 'outrages upon personal dignity, in particular humiliating and degrading treatment, rape, enforced prostitution and any form of indecent assault'. Article 5, paragraph 2a specifies that women who are arrested, detained or interned 'shall be held in quarters separated from those of men and shall be under the immediate supervision of women except when members of a family are accommodated together'. In the event that it is not possible to provide separate quarters, it is essential in any event to provide separate sleeping places and conveniences. It should be noted that the foregoing provision refers both to civilians deprived of their freedom and to captured combatants. The Protocol goes even further than the International Covenant on Civil and Political Rights. Article 6, paragraph 4 specifies that 'the death penalty shall not be carried out on mothers of young children'.[24]

While these rights of women are detailed in the Geneva Conventions, not all governments have ratified the relevant conventions or protocols. And, even if a state has ratified the instruments, it is its prerogative to permit the International Committee of the Red Cross entry into its territory.

In reality, civilians, including women and children, are often the first victims of conflicts. Fleeing one's home or taking refuge in a displaced persons' camp is not necessarily protection from physical attacks. Moreover, for internally displaced women, even more so than refugees, access to assistance, particularly food, shelter and health care, is often the primary protection problem encountered. In a number of countries, governments and/or resistance forces have used food as a weapon, and impeded efforts to provide international assistance to civilians under their control.

In Angola, both government and rebel forces (UNITA) are reported to have deliberately starved displaced persons and to have planted mines to prevent farming or the possibility of subsistence. In Mozambique, according to well-documented accounts, the rebel group RENAMO has massacred, maimed, or mutilated over 100,000 persons and used food as a weapon to bring civilians under control. In the Sudan and Ethiopia, food repeatedly has been used as a weapon by government and rebel forces, causing the deaths of hundreds of thousands of displaced persons.[25]

In Liberia, government troops attacked a UN compound housing internally displaced persons, which led the Secretary-General to evacuate all UN personnel from the country.

Where a government or the resistance movement in control of a territory is unwilling to permit international observers into the area to monitor abuses or provide assistance, the international community can do little to provide protection. Often, governments fail or refuse to request assistance on the grounds that it could undermine their state sovereignty. This applies particularly when governments themselves are the cause of the displacements or when they want to conceal from the international community the extent of abuse within their countries.

Recognizing the seriousness of the problems encountered by internally displaced persons, there has been growing interest within the UN and among governments and NGOs to explore new approaches. Two international conferences – on refugees, returnees and displaced persons in Africa (SARRED) and Central America (CIREFCA) – documented the inadequacy of current mechanisms. The SARRED meeting recommended that 'mechanisms should be examined by the UN concerning relief programmes for internally displaced persons'.

The Secretary-General, having made such an examination, authorized the UN

Development Programme field representatives to be the focal points for co-ordinating relief to the internally displaced. A system-wide review of the UN's responsibility regarding assistance for refugees, returnees and displaced persons began in the spring of 1991 as a result of a General Assembly resolution. The UN Commission on Human Rights requested that the Secretary-General include protection issues in this review. The UN Commission on the Status of Women further requested that particular attention be paid to the situation of women and children.

STEPS TO BE TAKEN TO IMPROVE PROTECTION FOR INTERNALLY DISPLACED WOMEN

- Bring greater public attention to the plight of internally displaced persons, focusing on the situation of women and their dependants.

- Engage human rights institutions, including the UN human rights system and NGOs, along with relief development agencies, in exposing cases where governments refuse to provide food, clothing, medicine and other essentials to their displaced populations.

- Develop standards for the protection of internally displaced persons. These standards should spell out the responsibilities of governments, opposition forces and the international community.

While these reviews were underway, some practical measures were taken to facilitate the assistance and security of internally displaced persons in Iraq. The Security Council passed Resolution 688 calling on Iraq not to hinder the provision of assistance to internally displaced persons inside its territory. Following passage of the resolution, several countries, including the US, UK and France, established a security zone within Iraq and built camps for Kurds who had taken refuge in the mountains bordering Turkey. The UN also negotiated its access to internally displaced persons so that multilateral assistance could be provided. All coalition troops were moved out of Northern Iraq in July 1991, but they remained on alert in Southern Turkey to return if Iraqi forces attacked the Kurds. In the meantime, UNHCR assumed responsibility for providing assistance to the Kurds in Northern Iraq. Although it is too soon to identify the ramifications of these activities, they may spell some new hope for addressing the desperate situation of internally displaced persons.

CONCLUSION □ The protection of refugee and displaced women should be of the highest priority to the international community. As seen from this discussion, protection is a concept that encompasses many aspects of a refugee's life from physical safety to legal rights. A key condition of effective protection is access to the assistance needed to survive within a refugee and displaced persons' context. The next chapter spells out in greater detail the various assistance needs of the uprooted women and their dependants.

1   UNHCR, nd, UNHCR.
2   Annick Roulet-Billard, 1989, p. 25.
3   A.M. 'Eyewitness: Maria's Story' *Refugees*, 1982.
4   John Tenhula, 1991, p. 69.
5   'A Tale of Horror' *Refugees*, Vol. 65, p. 25, 1989.
6   Dao Tu Khuong, in Diana Miserez (ed.) (1988), p. 24.
7   Roberta Aitchison, in *Cultural Survival Quarterly*, Vol. 8, No. 2, p. 26, Summer 1984.
8   Anders Johnsson, 1988.
9   UNHCR, nd.
10 Women's Commission for Refugee Women and Children 1990.
11 Gail and Mohn Sheehy, *Parade*, 27 August 1989.
12 Lawyers Committee for Human Rights, 1987 p. 73.
13 Rita Giacaman, *Journal of Refugee Studies*, Vol. 2, No. 1, p. 142, 1989.
14 Ibid.
15 UNHCR (Technical Support Service) 1990c, p. 2.

16 Dutch Ministry of Social Affairs and Labour, 1984.
17 Amnesty International, 1991, p. 49.
18 Elizabeth Ferris, 1990, p. 2.
19 UNHCR, 1990e, p. 5.
20 Inger Agger, *Journal of Traumatic Stress*, Vol. 2., No, 3, 1989.

21 UNHCR, nd.
22 African Training and Research Center for Women, 1986 p. 22.
23 Lance Clark, 1989.
24 Francoise Krill, 1985.
25 Roberta Cohen, 1990.

Central American woman with 2 children.

⁴ ASSISTANCE: FRIEND OR FOE?

Life in Tendelti is unimaginably harsh. The water is nauseously turbid and smelly. The food is insubstantial and unappetizing. The straw hovels they live in are little more than raffia mats propped up by sticks, no protection against the torrential rain storms which come every other day. But the women of Tendelti are finding ways to live there with the 4,000 children under the age of seven.[1]

ALMOST HALF OF THE WORLD'S refugees are totally dependent on international assistance for the basic needs of food, shelter, water and health care. For new arrivals, this situation is not surprising. Refugees fleeing their home countries are usually without material resources when they arrive in a neighbouring country. The clothing on their backs and perhaps a small bundle of belongings are often all that they have been able to bring with them. They may arrive in poor health, malnourished and/or disabled, having experienced famine in their countries of origin and long treks through hazardous terrain.

That large numbers of refugees continue to be dependent on international assistance is more disturbing. In many countries, they remain in care-and-maintenance camps long after the emergency is over, denied opportunities to work or access to training or income-producing activities. They must rely on food rations, clothing and shelter as provided by international donors. Of a bare substistence nature even at the best of times, during periods of financial strain the assistance package in a number of countries has been found inadequate to meet even the basic nutritional needs of the population. Further, there is often little co-ordination among the various sections of assistance – health, education, skills training, for example – to better encourage independence.

Refugee women are affected in three ways by this international assistance system. As the principal beneficiaries of assistance, they and their children suffer from its inadequacies. Unable to obtain employment and often denied participation in training or income-generation programmes, they cannot provide for their families without international assistance. And, finally, they are seldom consulted about the programmes in place or permitted to participate actively in the implementation of projects ostensibly designed to assist them.

This chapter considers the assistance issues encountered by refugee and displaced women, using information, largely anecdotal, gleaned from researchers' field visits to refugee camps and the reports of individuals and groups working with refugee women.

ACCESS TO FOOD, WATER AND NON-FOOD ITEMS ☐ The principal cause of mortality in refugee and displaced persons' camps is malnutrition. Lack of food itself kills, and is a major contributor to death from a number of diseases. Malnourished people are more susceptible to disease and are more difficult to cure when they are ill. Malnourished women who are pregnant or lactating are unable to provide sufficient nutrients to enable their children to survive. In addition to food problems, poor sanitation and contaminated water supplies contribute to high death rates in many refugee situations. People denied such basic items as shelter, clothing and cooking utensils are also at risk of disease.

Iraqi woman making bread.

According to the UNHCR Handbook for Emergencies, the average food ration must provide the following amounts of energy: at least 1,500 Kcal (6.3MJ) for initial survival and over 2,000 Kcal (8.4MJ) for longer-term maintenance. The diet must satisfy protein and basic vitamin requirements and pay particular attention to locally prevalent nutritional deficiencies. A typical daily ration would be built around a staple food, which provides the bulk of the energy and protein requirements (for example, cereal 350–400g), an energy-rich food (such as oil 20–40g), and a protein-rich food (for example, beans 50g).[2]

Two types of ration distribution are used. The preferred method is dry ration distribution where the refugees take the ration home and prepare the food as they wish; this method also requires distribution of cooking pots, fuel and utensils. The second is cooked food distribution where central kitchens are established and the refugees collect meals already prepared.

While the cooked food distribution can be culturally more problematic, it is used under emergency circumstances when individual cooking facilities and equipment are not available. Communal cooking continues over the longer term in some camps. In some cases, this process serves to undermine family structures and roles since it changes traditional responsibilities for provision and preparation of food. With full participation of women in decisions on communal cooking, however, it can serve the purpose of increasing community cohesion:

Two large kitchens served the entire camp, and nearly all of the women participated in the food preparation and distribution. They served on teams which rotated on a daily basis. The community kitchen promoted community living and ensured equal access to a good diet for all. Representatives, chosen from teams, participated in the menu planning and evaluation sessions. These sessions took into consideration such concerns as: the customs and preferences of the people, special dietary needs, seasonal availability of local as well as home-grown fruits and vegetables, nutritional standards, and budgetary constraints. Two of the women were also responsible for the twice-weekly purchasing of perishable foods.

The aim was to provide a well-balanced diet that was acceptable to the people, adaptable to special needs (the elderly, pregnant and lactating women, children and the infirm) and yet simple enough to be transferable to future living situations outside the camp. For this reason, expensive items such as meat, fish and chicken were included in the diet only in limited amounts.[3]

Equal access to food and non-food items is a key issue for refugee and displaced women and children. Decisions about food distribution are generally made by international organizations and host countries in consultation with the male leaders of the camps. Yet, these male leaders may have little understanding of the needs and circumstances of those who cook the food or feed their families, that is, the women. As a result, the food distribution procedures and contents may be inappropriate. Food that is inconsistent with the refugees' and displaced persons' dietary traditions may be provided. Or, food offered may require preparation that cannot readily be accomplished in the camp setting. These problems are further compounded by cultural practices among some refugee and displaced populations that require that men be fed first. Where supplies are limited, women and children may not receive adequate food.

The predominance of male-dominated food distribution is clearly at odds with traditional patterns in which women play a lead role in food production. The World

PHOTO: UNHCR/A. HOLLMANN

Afghan men and food aid.

Bank reports that 70 per cent of the food grown in developing countries is produced by women. Although the pattern differs somewhat by region, women in developing countries are also typically involved in animal husbandry, activities aimed at storing food, selling and exchanging produce, and the preparation and cooking of food. In Africa, women are often the sole cultivators, whereas in Asia joint cultivation by spouses is more typical. In Latin America, women tend to take over cultivation when their husbands seek employment in the cities to supplement agricultural work.[4]

In some circumstances, food distributed through male networks has been diverted to resistance forces or for sale on the black market, with women and children suffering as a result. In other situations, food has been used as a weapon by both government and resistance forces which have blocked distribution to civilian populations, particularly displaced persons. In

still other cases, male distributors of food and other items have required sexual favours in exchange for the assistance goods.

Distributing food directly to women can reduce some of these problems. In the camps along the Thai–Cambodian border, for example, the UN Border Relief Operation (UNBRO) provided rations to women and girls over the age of eight for redistribution or sale, as necessary, to cover the needs of the camps. This policy succeeded in reducing the diversion of food to the military. It required some changes over time, however, because families with few or no girls tended to be disadvantaged in comparison with those with a larger number of female members.

In many situations involving refugees and displaced persons, food rations are inadequate to meet the needs of the population even when there is no diversion. Currently, about seven million refugees are dependent on food aid provided by UNHCR and the World Food Programme (WFP). Recent surveys show that an average of 10–15 per cent of refugee children under the age of five are malnourished, with rates in some countries as high as 30 per cent. By UNHCR's estimate, this means that 150,000 to 225,000 refugee children are malnourished. By comparison, malnutrition rates among other populations range from two to five per cent in South-East Asia, South-West Asia and Central America, five to ten per cent in Africa. Famine level malnutrition rates are 20 to 30 per cent.[5]

Inadequacies in the basic food ration are largely to blame. WFP is facing major shortfalls in food supplies at the same time that a budgetary crisis at UNHCR impedes its ability to cushion ration cuts by purchasing additional food. The basic ration in a number of locations has been cut both in calories and content. As a result, outbreaks of such diseases as scurvy and pellagra have been reported in Ethiopia, Angola, Malawi, Swaziland, and Zimbabwe. Increases in childhood malnutrition have been reported in these countries as well as in Hong Kong, Mexico and Thailand.

Among adults, women are particularly susceptible to problems arising from inadequacies in the basic ration. They are particularly affected by deficiencies in iron, calcium, iodine and Vitamin C. Pregnant women and lactating mothers are very much at risk. For example, pregnant women who are anaemic run the risk of a fatal haemorrhage during childbirth. Supplementary feeding programmes may be essential to maintain even a modicum of good health for these women and their children.

Improved techniques for obtaining clean water are another essential need. Women in refugee and displaced persons camps, like many other women in developing countries, spend a great deal of time collecting water; containers that are too heavy or inconveniently located pumps can make this task more difficult and time-consuming. Similarly, collecting fuel for cooking and heating is a task for which women are generally responsible. In a refugee or displaced persons' context, however, efforts to find firewood can not only be time-consuming (if located at some distance from the camps) but dangerous (if located in mine-infested areas or the site of conflict).

STEPS TO BE TAKEN TO IMPROVE NUTRITIONAL STATUS

- Include refugee women in all decisions about food distribution.

- Designate women as the initial point of contact for emergency food distribution, particularly where necessary to prevent diversion of food from the civilian population.

- Monitor regularly the health status of women and children as well as the capacity to provide a nutritionally balanced diet and to identify problems in the food ration or its distribution. Where nutritional deficiencies or declining nutritional status is detected, immediate steps should be taken to increase the calories or improve the nutritional content of the rations.

- Give greater priority to breastfeeding in all refugee and displaced persons' settings. Milk powder should not be distributed in such a manner that it encourages mothers to use it as a substitute for breastfeeding.

The distribution of and use of milk powder for infant feeding presents a further problem in refugee and displaced persons's camps. Refugee mothers who, due to their own poor nutrition, are unable to lactate, use milk powder. Because donors find it costly to store, milk powder is donated as part of their foreign aid and is, therefore, often accessible. Its use, however, can be the cause of numerous health problems that do not occur when mothers breastfeed. As a WHO pamphlet states, 'in many developing countries...poor women in mainly urban areas, in unsanitary conditions, with unclean water and insufficient money to buy enough breast-milk substitute, are weaning their babies too early, with disastrous results',[6] Such conditions are common to refugee camps. When mixed with non-sterile water, milk powder can lead to severe diarrhoea and even death.

ACCESS TO APPROPRIATE HEALTH CARE ☐ Refugee and displaced women's and children's access to health care services is important both for their own health and for the welfare of the broader community. Women as we have noted, typically bear responsibility for all family chores, fuel-gathering, water collection, child care and cooking. Should a woman become incapacitated due to ill health – or even die – she can no longer perform these tasks, and thereby her family is put at risk. Women are also the prime providers of health care to their family, whose health will be related directly to the mother's knowledge or interest in promoting a healthy environment and taking preventative actions against disease.

HEALTH PROBLEMS OF REFUGEE AND DISPLACED WOMEN Refugee and displaced women and children face similar health problems to those of other women and children in developing countries, but many of them are compounded by the refugee experience. Nutritional problems have been discussed. Refugee women may suffer physical disabilities resulting from their refugee experience, perhaps as victims of mine explosions, for example. Loss of limbs is not uncommon both in flight and during stays in camps.

Once the emergency phase is over, a leading cause of death among those women who are of child-bearing age is complications from pregnancies. Lack of training of midwives, septic abortions, unsanitary conditions during birth, septic instruments, poor lighting during deliveries, and frequency of pregnancies all create difficulties. Problems are compounded by high birth rates in many camps, rates that sometimes exceed traditional birth rates prior to flight. Spiralling birth rates result from a variety of factors: for example, means of birth control may not be available or usable in the refugee setting, refugee groups that have lost significant numbers of children may want to rebuild their population, and cultural and social values may encourage large families.

Because women are generally responsible for collecting and storing water, they are particularly susceptible to water-borne diseases. Contaminated water is responsible for causing such illnesses as typhoid, cholera, dysentery and infectious hepatitis. In addition, women are at risk of infection by disease carried by insects that breed or feed near water: for example, sleeping sickness, malaria, yellow fever and river blindness. They also risk infection from diseases transmitted through contact with water, such as worms and schistosomiasis. Measles and other diseases that particularly affect children, and which can be prevented through immunizations, are a too-frequent cause of death in the camps.

Health complications also often result from female genital mutilation (often referred to as circumcision), a practice in some parts of Africa and the Middle East that continues in the camps. Problems include: infections due to unsterile instruments, damage to adjacent organs, obstructed menstrual flow, painful intercourse, severe blood loss and obstetric complications.[7] Health workers are often insufficiently knowledgeable about the practice and consequences of female genital mutilation, and need training to recognize and treat symptoms. In addition, educational efforts are needed to inform the refugees and displaced persons of the health hazards of these practices. Traditional birth attendants should be a principal target of these efforts, and they should be informed of campaigns used elsewhere to reduce the incidence of female genital mutilation.[8]

In addition to physical health problems, some refugee and displaced women suffer mental health problems. Becoming a refugee involves many dislocations and abrupt changes in life. At a minimum, the women face emotional problems and difficulties in adjustment resulting from loss of family and community support. More serious mental health problems arising from torture and sexual abuse prior to or after flight, are not uncommon. As we have seen in the previous chapter, rape and abduction occur in many refugee situations. Depression and post-traumatic stress disorder often follow such experiences. Common symptoms experienced by survivors of traumatic events include anxiety, intrusive thoughts, disassociation or psychic numbing, hyper-alertness, and sleeping and eating disorders. The most serious mental health problems of refugees may manifest themselves in severe depressive, self-destructive, violent or disruptive behaviour, alcohol or drug abuse, and a high degree of psychosomatic illness.[9]

As one Afghan physcian stated:

Many women fall victim to depression or neurasthenia as a result of their loneliness and uprooting from their homes. Some come to see me only in order to obtain moral support and have someone with whom they can talk. They are happy to find a doctor who, like themselves, is a woman, and who speaks their language.[10]

Afghan woman with child seeing a doctor.

PHOTO: UNHCR/A. HOLLMAN

Although many refugee women have been raped, rape counselling programmes are few. Other mental health services are also lacking in most camps; nor are counselling programmes available for women who have undergone the trauma of dislocation.

CONSTRAINTS ON ACCESS TO SERVICES

In contrast to other sectors, refugees are sometimes advantaged relative to their neighbouring population's access to health care services. Special programmes may be implemented in the camps; expatriate physicians and nurses offer their services. Yet, access to health care is not universal in refugee settings. Groups that often find it difficult to gain access include internally displaced persons, who may be located in inaccessible or dangerous areas; returnees, who may be returning to areas where no health infrastructure remains; spontaneously settled refugees who are outside formal camp settings and reliant on host country facilities (to the extent they can legally use these services); and women and children, as described below.

Inappropriate or inaccessible health services can be obstacles to good health among refugee and displaced women and their families. The absence of female health practitioners has been one of the principal barriers to health care, particularly where cultural values prevent a woman from consultation, examination and treatment, or even being seen by a man who is not a member of her immediate family. Underutilization of health services by Afghan refugee women in Pakistan, and Cambodian women along the Thai–Cambodian border, for example, has been attributed to reluctance to be treated by male health personnel.

Failure to utilize the existing networks of female health practitioners in refugee communities has also caused a variety of problems. For example, a number of pro-grammes have trained refugee men to serve as medical assistants but then find that they leave the camps. Some seek resettlement abroad; others are conscripted to serve as medics in the military forces. By contrast, women health workers tend to be not only more appropriate practitioners but also more stable members of the community. As an assessment of one. programme along the Thai–Cambodian border found:

The [non-governmental organization] had been working in the refugee camp...for five years, trying to build up a refugee health care system. The main effort was training medics as primary health care providers. But each time a new crop of medics was trained, they disappeared.

At the same time, the Khmer Women's Association (KWA) was training women in literacy throughout the camp. The literacy programme included lessons on hygiene and nutrition. Each zone of the camp had a women's association office. The older women were in charge of the system. They represented the most stable elements of the camp population, having responsibility for their families, while their husbands were present in the camp only intermittently for 'rest and recuperation'.

The NGO focused on immediate medical needs and provided excellent curative care. By training Khmer medics, the agency's staff transferred skills and information to the refugee population, but neglected the social network that would have promoted health throughout the camp. It missed the opportunity to work with the KWA, strengthening their capacities to build a stable curative and preventive health system in the control of the refugees themselves.[11]

40

African woman spinning.

41

Recruitment of women to become health workers is thus essential to the operation of health services. UNHCR has recommended that at least 50 per cent of all health workers should be female. In order to meet that goal, however, some changes will be necessary in the operation of health services. Special efforts will be required to identify women within the refugee community, including traditional birth attendants, who have the trust and confidence of other refugee and displaced women. Agencies that place high value on English language skills and literacy in their refugee workers may need to change their criteria for recruitment of health workers if it appears that insufficient numbers of refugee and displaced women fit them. They may also need to redesign their training programmes to include an emphasis on the development of literacy skills. A further necessity is to develop mechanisms to convince male leaders that women should become health workers, particularly where there are cultural constraints on women taking employment outside the home. Recruitment of women as expatriate and host country staff also needs to be intensified, particularly in those posts involving supervision of refugee women staff and clinical services for women.

An additional problem relates to the types of services offered. Existing health services too often overlook female-specific needs; for example, gynaecological services are frequently inadequate. Basic needs, such as adequate cloth and washing facilities for menstruating women, are overlooked. Serious problems, such as vaginal infections and cervical cancer, go all but undetected. Counselling regarding sexually transmitted diseases is generally inadequate. Few if any programmes focus on the needs of adolescent girls even though early marriages and pregnancies are a reported cause of poor health.

Access to family planning information and devices is limited in most refugee camps, even where it is available to women in the host country (Pakistan, for example). In some cases, refugees and displaced persons are reluctant to practise birth control because of cultural constraints or unfamiliarity. One report cites the sensitivities of minority groups: 'family planning may be a particularly sensitive issue, especially where ethnic rivalry is the root cause of population dislocation; those displaced usually come from the minority ethnic groups'.[12] In a number of camps, Catholic agencies provide health services, including maternal and child health, and health education, but because of their own religious constraints they are unable to include family planning in their programmes.

The environment of the camps makes certain family planning techniques difficult to use. Storage space or privacy for use of some birth control devices may be absent. In some camps, birth control pills are provided on a monthly basis, but long queues at clinics may make it difficult to obtain refills; refugee women have also reported problems in having IUDs checked because of long waiting lists at clinics.

The use of depo-provera has become common in some family planning programmes. This drug, in common with some other birth control devices, can have serious side effects, including prolonged, excessive menstrual bleeding, mood swings and depression. Sufficient information, which would allow women to give informed consent for its use, is rarely given; this has created unfortunate consequences for family planning efforts. In Hong Kong, for example, women were given shots of depo-provera during a rubella epidemic in June 1988, but without adequate explanation, either of the reasons or the side effects. Subsequently, many Vietnamese women were reluctant to go to family planning clinics for fear that they would be given depo-provera without their consent.[13]

Logistical problems also impede access to health care. Inconvenient clinic hours may prevent women from going for health services or bringing their children; other time-consuming responsibilities limit women's flexibility. Also, clinics may be too far from home. Concerns about security also impede access: in some camps, women are reluctant to go to clinics because they must cross insecure areas to get there. In one camp in Hong Kong, passes to the clinic are issued by camp leaders who, in return, ask for bribes or sexual favours.

Since the treatment of some diseases, such as tuberculosis, requires regular visits to health centres, these logistical problems create complications for follow-up. Some innovative programmes have been implemented to deal with this access problem. In Pakistan, for example, mobile health units travel from village to village in remote areas to ensure that refugee women and children receive health services.

Inappropriate design of health programmes is another impediment to their effective utilization. An emphasis on preventive programming supposedly dominates health care systems, but many programmes are still focused primarily on curative services. In many situations, men are the primary users of in-patient facilities. Some hospital beds are used almost exclusively by soldiers who have returned to their families in refugee and displaced persons' camps because they have been wounded or suffer from such diseases as malaria. While this fact presents a set of issues that are outside the scope of this book, it is significant for this purpose because such use of health care services is often at the expense of preventive efforts that would improve the health status of women and children.

MODEL HEALTH PROGRAMMES Model health programmes for refugee women exist in a number of locations. UNRWA's health programme for Palestinian refugees combines a public health approach with special provisions for women:

UNRWA focuses on preventive and community health programmes which are provided through a network of 104 health units with children and mothers as the major target group. The basic community health programme covers maternal and child health care, an expanded programme of immunization, school health services, supplementary feeding to assure satisfactory levels of nutrition, and environmental sanitation in the refugee camps (home for about one-third of the refugees registered with UNRWA). A family planning programme, including family life education, is offered in the Gaza Strip, Jordan and the Syrian Arab Republic. Health education classes for mothers are held at the Maternal and Child Health Centres (MCH). Women attending UNRWA activities and sewing centres are also given lectures by health education workers on personal hygiene and other topics related to healthy living.[14]

AVERAGE MONTHLY ATTENDANCE AT THE MCHCs	
Children aged below one year:	44,000
Children aged 1–2 years:	46,000
Children aged 2–3 years:	44,500
Pregnant women:	18,000

In response to high levels of infant mortality (150–170 deaths per 1,000 births) among refugees, the Somali government introduced the following programme:

The Refugee Health Unit (RHU) within the Ministry of Health was set up to administer and coordinate refugee health activities and set priorities and guidelines for health. Refugee women themselves have been involved in the health administration,

mainly as community health workers, Traditional Birth Attendants (TBAs) and nurses. Mother and Child Health Centres (MCH) have also been established in refugee camps, running maternity and infant clinics, immunization campaigns, and education programmes in personal hygiene, waste disposal and child care. Feeding centres distribute supplementary and specialized foods to pregnant and nursing mothers and to their other children who are malnourished.[15]

A displaced persons' camp in El Salvador established an effective health programme, after some false starts:

Many of the women were pregnant when they arrived. Initially, the camp was not equipped to handle deliveries within the camp. A number of the women delivered their own children or assisted others, but there was no recognized midwife in the group. Therefore, when labour started, women were taken to the maternity hospital in San Salvador (approximately 30 minutes by car over bumpy roads) for delivery and postpartum care. This arrangement was unsatisfactory to the women, as most were undocumented, had never been hospitalized, were unfamiliar with the city, were frightened and did not want to be left alone (a hospital regulation). They urged the medical staff and administration of the camp to allow them to remain within the camp for delivery where they would have the support of family and/or friends.

Within six months, the prenatal care programme was functional, and a group of interested health promoters had been trained to assist with routine examinations. They also supported the women through labour, delivery and the immediate postpartum phase. Hospital referrals continued to be utilized when requested by the woman, or when complications were anticipated or arose.

Initially, some of the women did not trust the health promoters and preferred to handle the delivery on their own, or perhaps with assistance of a friend or husband. Often they only advised the **clinic staff after the fact. Eventually, mutually agreeable arrangements were usually worked out; the woman was invited to come to the clinic at the start of labour. Two health promoters would be in attendance, but the presence of a family member or friend was also encouraged. Gradually, the health promoters became more proficient and confident, gaining valuable expertise for future work as village midwives. The women who were assisted became more confident and appreciative of the health promoters.[16]**

Dao Tu Khuong, a Vietnamese psychologist who worked as a UNHCR consultant, has developed the following recommendations to build a social support system for rape victims:

- *Reception and support committees* in all camps, whether arrival camps, like Pulau Bidong, transit camps, or refugee processing centres (RPCs). Such committees should have the following tasks:

  (1) to help women in daily camp life, through information, familiarization, support and protection;

  (2) to provide literacy courses;

  (3) to sensitize refugees to Western attitudes to women: different attitudes in the West towards the value of women, sexuality and the relative freedom in sexual behaviour in the man/woman relationship, the changing position of women in Western society;

  (4) to prepare for the process of adaptation of daily practical life, by means of films, documents, lectures, and meetings.

- *Psychological supports:* in all the camps, make available for those who wish to receive it psychological support offered by a woman of the same culture and language as the refugees. This last criterion is important to enable refugees to express themselves better and thus to recover some of their lost identity. This would create an area of confidence and security which would help recreate or re-establish a person-to-person relationship.[17]

STEPS TO BE TAKEN TO IMPROVE HEALTH CARE FOR REFUGEE WOMEN

- Emphasize a primary health care approach in all health programmes for refugees and displaced persons, with particular focus on preventive care.

- Assess all health programmes to ensure that they are appropriate for refugee and displaced women, and that women have equal access to their services.

- Require the full participation of refugee and displaced women in the planning and implementation of the health services.

- Require in contracts and agreements with institutions operating health programmes that at least 50 per cent of their health workers should be women. Increased efforts should be made to recruit and train women as health workers.

- Give high priority to ensuring that gynaecological services, birthing care, counselling regarding sexually transmitted diseases, and family planning programmes are available in all refugee and displaced persons' settings. Special attention should be paid to services needed by adolescent girls.

- Provide counselling and mental health services for refugee and displaced women and children, particularly for victims of torture, rape and other physical and sexual abuse.

EDUCATION AND SKILLS TRAINING □
The right to education is universal. The Universal Declaration of Human Rights states explicitly 'Everyone has the right to education. Education should be free, at least in the elementary and fundamental stage.'

CHILDHOOD EDUCATION The UN convention Relating to the Status of Refugees provides that: 'Contracting States shall accord to refugees the same treatment as is accorded to nationals with respect to elementary education.' The Executive Committee of the UNHCR has reaffirmed the fundamental right of refugee children to education and, in its 38th Session called upon all states, individually and collectively, to intensify their efforts to ensure that refugee children benefit from primary education. Yet the right to education continues to be curtailed.

Millions of refugee and displaced children are without education, even at the elementary level. In 1987, fewer than 500,000 of an estimated five million children receiving assistance from UNHCR were enrolled in schools. The education coverage is poor by comparison with either the surrounding host country population or the country of origin. A recent survey by UNHCR found that 29 per cent of refugee children of school age in Malawi were receiving education (in contrast to 62 per cent of the Malawian children and 49 per cent of the Mozambican children). Even lower proportions of refugee children were receiving education in the Sudan (9.5–14.4 per cent for Ethiopian refugees contrasted with 36 per cent for Ethiopia itself) and Pakistan (12.5 per cent for Afghan refugees contrasted with 18 per cent in Afghanistan and 47 per cent in Pakistan).

The situation for girls is particularly bad. In Pakistan, only about 8,000 Afghan girls are enrolled in school (out of a total enrolment of 125,000). This figure represents less than one-tenth of one per cent of the school age girls. A study of two camps in Somalia showed that approximately 4,000 children were enrolled in pri-

45

mary school, but only 40 per cent were in attendance, almost all of them boys. Because figures are not kept by gender in most locations, it is difficult to know how widespread is the lack of access to schooling for refugee girls. According to the Economic Commission for Africa, 'the proportion of females enrolled for primary schooling is even lower in the spontaneously settled urban and semi-urban communities, where refugees compete with nationals for the same educational facilities'.

Even where refugee children have access to schools, the classes may be seriously overcrowded. Teacher shortages are a further problem. As reported by the Economic Commission of Africa:

Refugee teachers often lack adequate training, and the numbers of trained national personnel are inadequate for even national needs. Female teachers are often under-represented in refugee

schools, sometimes because few women had access to education in the country of origin. Materials are also in short supply, and a curious mixture of textbooks and teaching materials of different origins is found in refugee schools — whatever happens to be available rather than that which is suitable.'[18]

When financial crises occur, education is often among the first activities to be cut. Priority is given to life-sustaining projects. The long-term effects of such cutbacks can result in a debilitated school system. In discussing the financial crisis confronting UNHCR in recent years, the head of its Programme Management Service stated:

We are now reaching the stage where some budget reductions may simply prove too severe to sustain.... In the educational sector, substantial cutbacks in

African children with school books.

the construction of new facilities and provision of materials will mean that many refugee children are denied access to schooling.[19]

A major exception to the education record for refugees has been that of the Palestinians. Initially, no provision had been made for UNRWA to administer education programmes, but the longstanding nature of the refugee problem made it clear that schools were needed. In 1948, only 27 per cent of all school age children received education but over time the coverage increased dramatically. The initial preponderance of male pupils (74 per cent in 1951) also disappeared over time, and the female/male ratio now is about equal. Today, UNRWA spends about half its total budget (US$255 million for 1991) on education, running 631 elementary and junior secondary schools for 358,000 pupils as well as eight vocational and teacher training centres for 5,000 students.

Palestinian refugee women play an important part in this education programme. Some 99 per cent of the agency's 18,600 employees are Palestinian refugees and 12,600 of them are employed in the education programme, including more than 10,000 as teachers, just under half of whom are women. Palestinian refugee women also hold many of the key posts in the school system which UNRWA runs with technical assistance from UNESCO. In the 1988–89 school year, 286 of the agency's 608 head teachers and 36 of the 62 assistant head teachers were women.

This education system is remarkable not only because it achieves good results, (Palestinian schoolchildren have traditionally shown a great enthusiasm for learning) but also because it follows the national school curriculae of four countries, Jordan, Syria, Lebanon and Egypt (for schools in the Gaza Strip). UNRWA has continued to operate its schools whenever possible despite war, civil strife, curfews and forced closures.

SECONDARY AND UNIVERSITY EDUCATION

Opportunities for secondary and university education for refugees are limited in almost all locations. In many countries, refugees' access to secondary education is subject to special regulation by the host country. In Tanzania, for example, the admission of refugee children to secondary schools is based on the non-citizen quota allocation of two per cent of the places available in Form I. Refugees in Somalia have some access to post-primary formal education but it depends on competing with the local community for admission. The chances of success are limited in both cases, particularly for girls.

UNHCR operates scholarship programmes that allow a small number of refugees to obtain higher education. A report in 1984 of the secondary and tertiary educational scholarship programme showed discrimination against women; scholarships generally went to single, male students. Most educational scholarships do not provide support for dependants. Women with children find the available resources inadequate to support their families; they are therefore less likely to apply.

The longest-operating school for higher education for refugee women is the Ramallah Women's Training Centre, established by UNRWA in 1962 as a boarding college for Palestinian refugees. Since then, 6,800 refugee women have graduated from the teacher and vocational training courses. The centre offers places to 722 post-secondary students from the West Bank and Gaza. The teacher training programme produces elementary school teachers; the vocational training programme provides other marketable skills: dressmaking, hairdressing, nutrition and home management, and secretarial and office practice.

The curriculum has tended to coincide with community concepts about appropriate work for women, but the centre has also sought to break new ground. It now accepts married students with children, for example, in recognition of the need for two-income families. It has also adapted its rules as a result of the *intifada* and the closure of the school for a two-year period. As one student stated:

The *intifada* has changed many of the customs which the community traditionally imposed on women. I came to the centre in order to pursue my studies and get a college certificate. These certificates have become a 'weapon' aiding women in their lives. In view of the difficult economic situation we are facing, I need to work in order to help my husband, and to ensure a decent life for our children.[20]

Women refugees are also accepted at UNRWA's other vocational and teacher training centres. Some of them have even ventured into traditional male preserves, training as surveyors, construction technicians, in architectural drafting, engineering and electronics.

SKILLS AND LITERACY TRAINING FOR ADULT WOMEN
Refugee situations often call for new skills and occupations for women. Many skills that women bring with them are not immediately or directly relevant to their experiences in refugee camps or settlements. Although many of their skills are transferable, refugee and displaced women often need training to undertake new roles to support themselves and their families. Education and skills training provide numerous benefits, as reported in the NGO Consultation on Refugee Women:

- increasing a woman's income-earning potential, thus fostering self-sufficiency;

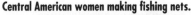
Central American women making fishing nets.

- furthering the ability of a woman to have some measure of control within the community in which she lives;

- providing skills which will be useful when, and if, the refugee returns home;

- enhancing the likelihood of resettlement;

- alleviating the oppressive monotony of camp life; and

- providing a measure of self-respect that may have been lost through years of unproductive exile.[21]

Refugee and displaced women face many of the same impediments to education and skills training as do children, namely inadequate resources, teachers and classes. In addition, women face other barriers. Cultural constraints sometimes prevent them from accepting work or undertaking training that takes them out of the household. Their culture may also restrict the type of work considered to be appropriate for females. Practical problems also constrain enrolment, including a need for child day-care, and lack of time and energy after household work and/or jobs as a wage earner. Also, many skills training programmes assume some level of prior education, most notably in terms of literacy. Refugee and displaced women may not qualify for such programmes, having been discriminated against in their country of origin in so far as obtaining elementary education is concerned.

STEPS TO BE TAKEN TO IMPROVE EDUCATION AND SKILLS TRAINING

- Reaffirm the right of all refugee and displaced children to primary education.

- Assess educational programmes and make changes, as needed, to ensure that girls have equal access to these programmes.

- Establish educational and training programmes for refugee and displaced women in proportion to their numbers within the refugee and displaced population.

- Ensure the full participation of refugee and displaced women in the development and implementation of these programmes.

Other constraints relate to the design and contents of training programmes. In some cases, courses have been too far removed from the everyday life activities of the refugee women and have therefore appeared irrelevant to their needs. Some vocational training activities have focused on skills that are not marketable in the refugee context. One evaluation of these programmes recommended that: 'Training should be linked directly to concrete productive goals. For the majority of women refugees, it is more effective to combine training with the production of goods and/or services from the outset, rather than on training which is intended to lead to income earning at a later date, when training is completed.'[22]

Despite these constraints, programmes designed to redress illiteracy among refugees, including women and girls, have often met with great enthusiam and success. In Honduras, for example, over 90 per cent of the refugees who arrived at one camp were illiterate. Refugee teachers were able to reduce this to 20 per cent through a camp literacy project.

In Somalia, a Family Education Programme which aimed to provide skills and augment income was established in 1984, with enrolment of about 8,000 women per year. It was modelled after a programme designed for Somali women in both rural and urban areas. Activities included training in tailoring, handicrafts, home improvement, health and hygiene, child care, nutrition and administration as well as literacy and numeracy. Training covers

PHOTO: UNHCR/Y. MÜLLER

African refugees.

a 12-month period, divided into three separate courses for four months each. Students receive a certificate on successful completion of the programme, but it is not recognized nationally and does not qualify them for further training or employment. Day-care centres, catering for 4,800 children under five, enabled mothers to participate. About 70 per cent of enrollees completed the courses.

In Angola, Botswana and Zambia, World University Service and the SWAPO Women's Solidarity Campaign produced adult education packs designed by and for women. Starting with issues relevant to women, such as pregnancy and nutrition, the materials use pictures and words to help women to increase control over their lives. The packs help develop new skills and confidence, as well as provide literacy in the English language.

C ONCLUSION ☐ Improving protection and assistance programmes for refugee and displaced women is an important first step in helping them resume their normal lives. As the next chapter will show, however, further efforts are needed if they are to become financially independent of these assistance efforts.

1 Paul Vallely, quoted in *Refugees*, Vol. 23, 1985, p. 35.
2 UNHCR, 1982.
3 Sr Margaret Jane Kling, (1989) in Ninette Kelly, 1989, p. 110.
4 Margaret Snyder, pp. 4–5.
5 UNHCR, 1990b.
6 See UNICEF, 1986, pp. 177–84.
7 Ninette Kelly, 1989, pp. 30–31.
   See UNICEF, 1986, pp. 177–84.
8 See, for example, the work of the Inter-African Committee on Traditional Practices Affecting the Health of Women and Children.
9 Lewin/ICF and Refugee Policy Group, 1990, p. 12.
10 Annick Billard, in *Refugees* vol. 2, 1983, p. 28.
11 Mary B. Anderson and Peter J. Woodrow, 1989, p. 24.

12 African Training and Research Centre for Women, 1986, p. 41.
13 Women's Commission for Refugee Women and Children, 1990; and UNHCR (Technical Support Service), 1990.
14 *Palestine Refugees Today*, No. 111, July 1985, pp. 6–7.
15 African Training and Research Centre for Women, 1986, p. 38.
16 Kling, in Ninette Kelly, 1989.
17 Khuong, in Diana Miserez (ed.), 1988, pp. 35–6.
18 African Training and Research Centre for Women, 1986, p. 44.
19 *Refugees*, Vol. 73, 1990, p. 8.
20 *Palestine Refugees Today*, No. 127, 1990, p. 3.
21 Ninette Kelly, 1989.
22 Eve Hall, 1988, p. 37.

5 TOWARDS GREATER SELF-SUFFICIENCY

Parwin is the oldest widow in the widow's camp of Nasir Bagh in Pakistan, where she lives together with 300 families of refugee widows and their children. Her age has allowed Parwin to ask for work in the name of the other women, so that they can purchase those articles which are not included in the general aid distribution. A project set up by a voluntary agency supplies these refugee widows with the necessary material for quilt-making which it then purchases from them. Parwin and the other refugee widows feel that this is a first step towards self-sufficiency, and that they would be able, given the opportunity, to undertake many more income-generating activities.[1]

A BASIC NEED OF MANY REFUGEE WOMEN, particularly heads of households, is sufficient income to support their families. The extent to which women in this situation are economic resources has often been underestimated. While household strategies for economic survival differ greatly, women in all situations play an important economic role.

The strategies vary depending on family composition, existing work opportunities, refugee and host country cultural constraints, and other factors. As one study noted:

Very poor people often adopt one of two strategies for survival. Either they become totally reliant on one source; a patron, an employer or, with refugees, a government feeding programme, or they cobble together a livelihood out of bits, improvising here, migrating there, fitting together a sequence of seasonal work to secure more or less adequate flows of food round the year.[2]

Especially in poorer families, the ability to engage in diverse economic activities can be crucial in enabling the family to survive. Refugee women in developing countries (like their host, national counterparts) are an integral part of the family's economic activities whether those entail assisting in food production, marketing goods or providing services such as cooking and laundry for other family members who are engaged in wage labour.

ECONOMIC ACTIVITIES ☐ The main component of initial household survival strategies, especially for woman-headed households, is the food ration. Most newly arrived refugees rely on rations as the key to survival during the first few weeks or months. If there are no opportunities to replace rations with other sources of income, either in cash or in kind, refugees may remain dependent on them for years.

Theoretically, there are a number of ways that refugees can supplement their household income. These include: employment in the local economy or with assistance agencies; agricultural activities; bartering; establishment of trades or small businesses; and participation in skills-training programmes and formal income-generation projects.

Refugees weigh several considerations when deciding what economic strategy to pursue. An important factor is the extent to which any activity will help obtain a *secure* source of income (either in cash or in kind) which enables them to survive. Lack of a safety net or financial cushion allows refugees only a small margin for financial risk-taking. As shown in development studies, a small farmer will not use a new variety of plant until it has proved to be reliable. A parallel can be drawn to the refugees' reluctance to give up ration cards even if a job without rations might provide them with more income.

Refugees also take into account their hopes and prospects for repatriation and resettlement; most anticipate a return to their country of origin. Generally, they prefer not to commit significant resources to a project in the country of asylum, particularly if it calls for a long period of commitment, even if the investment could provide a considerable return after a number of years. Typically, income, if not used for survival, will be invested in portable products such as animals or gold.

If the principal goal of a refugee is resettlement in a third country, other strategies may be attractive. For example, a refugee seeking resettlement may prefer to work for a voluntary agency from the desired resettlement country; a woman may accept a job as a domestic for an expatriate worker if she believes that this could lead to a recommendation for re-settlement in a third country; and others hoping for resettlement may enrol in skills-training or English language programmes in the hopes of increasing their chances.

The previous education and skill levels of the refugees also affect the strategies they pursue. An individual who engaged in a trade or performed skilled labour may find it possible to work in the local economy, whereas a professional, such as a lawyer, may find few outlets in the country of first asylum. A refugee who speaks the language of expatriate agency staff will find it much easier to obtain employment with the agencies that operate in her or his area because of the ability to communicate.

Finally, culture constrains choices as to appropriate strategies, particularly with regard to women's economic options. Women refugees whose culture generally prohibits employment outside the home will attempt to pursue strategies that permit them to work within their household compounds.

The economic activities of refugee households fall into the following categories detailed here.

EMPLOYMENT IN THE LOCAL ECONOMY OR WITH ASSISTANCE AGENCIES

Refugees often seek jobs in the local economies of their host countries. At times, they are given official permission to engage in such labour; in other situations, they work without formal authorization.

Refugee women, in common with other women in developing countries, most typically find employment in the informal sector of the economy. In general, refugee women who work in the local economy are within the service sector. For example, it is not uncommon to find a refugee woman supporting her family through her earnings as a domestic. These jobs are often a cornerstone in the household survival strategy for an extended family.

Assistance agencies are an important source of employment for refugees in developing countries. Typically these positions go to younger men who have the language skills to communicate with and relate to the expatriate staff in charge. These positions often offer a higher level of financial compensation than is usually available to refugees in the local market, relatively interesting, non-manual labour (though the employees often feel they are overqualified for the position), more security, higher status, and other benefits such as an increased chance for resettlement to a third country.

For refugee women the primary area of employment with assistance agencies is in the health sector. In several cultures, as already noted, it is more appropriate for women to seek medical advice from and be examined by women rather than men. The women employed by assistance agencies' health sectors work in supplementary feeding programmes, as traditional birth attendants, in mother/child health programmes, as home visitors, particularly in public health education and outreach, as translators, and so on. The second largest sector for employment is 'women's projects', including income-generating activities.

AGRICULTURAL ACTIVITIES Most refugees in developing countries are from rural areas. Prior to their flight the majority of them were involved in some kind of subsistence agricultural activities including crops and/or animals. It is not uncommon to hear refugees claim that their problems would be solved if they were to receive either land to farm or animals to tend, arguing that provision of these resources would eliminate the need for international assistance.

One strategy for attaining economic self-reliance, most commonly pursued in Africa and the People's Republic of China, is the creation of rural agricultural settlements for refugees. The primary goal is that refugees will become self-sufficient through agricultural activities. Refugee families receive plots of land to farm and can then, to some degree, reconstruct a life similar to the one they left behind.

Agricultural opportunities also exist in areas where large-scale rural settlements are not possible. Instead of creating rural settlements, the emphasis is on developing gardens next to the dwelling or compound; women are often involved in tending garden plots. These plots enable refugees to raise vegetables, either to supplement their diet or, if they choose, to sell to earn some extra cash.

MARKET ACTIVITIES Many refugees with no source of cash income have goods which the family can barter for other

Southeast Asian woman in a vegetable garden.

PHOTO: UNHCR/A. HOLLMAN

goods or sell in the camp or local markets. Small household goods or jewellery brought from home are common items of value in the markets. Basic food rations are bartered if no other resources are available.

These market activities can help upgrade refugees' standard of living or save them from having to buy goods on the open market. They may also be a way to secure some small cash income or products for the household. Rarely would a refugee family be able to become self-reliant through this activity alone, but it can be the difference between bare survival and an acceptable standard of living.

TRADES AND SMALL BUSINESSES

Skilled refugees often wish to use their skills in the host country, while others wish to learn skills that will help them generate income. Within refugee camps and settlements, as well as in neighbouring villages and cities, there may be need for such skilled workers as bakers, mechanics, cobblers, tailors, and others.

While some skilled refugees are successful in re-establishing themselves in business, others need assistance. Refugees may flee their countries at short notice, frequently travelling very far on foot, and those with skills are often unable to bring their tools of trade, without which they must work as unskilled labourers or remain dependent on assistance. In Pakistan, one agency estimated that over 10 per cent of the approximately 2.8 to 3 million refugees were in this situation.[3]

■NCOME-GENERATING PROJECTS □

Special projects have been implemented to address cultural constraints imposed on women who sought work outside the home. UNRWA, for instance, runs a modest programme of grants for income-generating projects in co-ordination with an NGO, to assist families to establish workshops or small businesses with start-up capital and initial support from a social worker. In Gaza, about 26 per cent of those employed in such projects are women. In the West Bank, the figure is as high as 44 per cent. Examples of projects started in the West Bank and Gaza Strip include a chicken farm, carpentry shop, car repair shop, and enterprises involving fattening calves and raising dairy cows. UNRWA also runs a small credit-based scheme to aid some of the poorest 152,000 refugees who qualify as 'special hardship cases'. About half the families in this category are headed by women.

Activities of income-generating projects often focus on what are perceived as traditional women's activities. In Sudan, for example, such projects for refugee women have included handicrafts, ceramics and soap-making. Handicraft projects are the major income-generating activity for refugee women in Pakistan. Following an agreement signed in 1985 between UNHCR and the Pakistani government to promote self-help activities, a number of projects were implemented in refugee villages. Some met with opposition from the male leadership but they were able to establish themselves by respecting 'purdah' (the separation of female and male activities in public), and focusing on particularly vulnerable women, such as widows without any other form of support.[4]

A number of problems have affected the success of these income-generation attempts. Generally, they targeted marginal economic activities such as handicrafts. Women have generally not been involved in some of the larger projects that focus on reforestation, infrastructure development, or agricultural activities. Interestingly, in many of the cultures from which the refugee women come, women are traditionally involved in these activities, raising questions about whether Western biases about women's traditional role may be constraining choices.

Palestinian woman sewing.

Few of the women's projects have led to long-term economic self-sufficiency for those involved. The programmes suffer from such problems as: lack of clarity regarding goals and objectives; lack of proper planning (skills assessment, market research, identification of appropriate participants); excessive administrative costs and/or inadequate funding; insufficient time for participants to become economically self-supporting; and inadequate consultation with the refugee community.[5]

These programmes do demonstrate, however, that refugee women are interested in increasing their incomes and will participate in economic activities outside the home if given the chance. And, some programmes have provided substantial support for the economic endeavours of refugee women. For example, the Port Sudan small-scale enterprise development programme provides loans, business training and advice. The Agency for Cooperation and Research in Development, ACORD, has a policy of reaching out to assist women refugees. About 40 per cent of their loans have gone to women-run enterprises.

The programme gives assistance by providing:

- tools and/or equipment on a hire-purchase basis. Credit ranges from between US$20–2,000, with a maximum repayment period of 20 months;

- loans for working capital, ranging from US$60–200 at a time, with a maximum repayment period of two months; and

- short-term loans, preferably to groups, for a maximum of US$15, which must be repaid in one month. These loans are primarily to buy basic raw material in bulk.

In addition, the programme provides workshops and market facilities for a small monthly rental. In the case of communal shelters for women vendors, rental is paid on a daily basis. There is a management consultancy service which, for a small fee based on the net income of the business, gives basic training in business management and monitors the progress of the enterprise for the period of the loan repayment.

The Austrian Relief Committee for Afghan Refugees (ARC) started a programme in 1984 to assist skilled refugees by providing the necessary tools. About 30 per cent of the beneficiaries have been women. ARC found that the women were skilled in dressmaking, carpet- and mat-weaving and handicraft production. In 1985, 308 refugee women received tools and equipment. The project has done much to improve the women's standard of living and increase their chances for economic self-sufficiency. A typical client:

Mrs Hafiya is 41 years old and migrated in 1982 from Kabul. She was living in a very old tent in Kababian Refugee Transit Village (RTV) with her husband and blind son before the Assistance to Skilled Afghan Refugees (ASAR) project made contact. She received ASAR's assistance in 1984 and works as a shoe repairer (she learned the skills from her husband). In the monitoring round in May 1985, it was observed that she had been able to pay the rent of a house at Rs 300/month and to buy some household items.[6]

The factors influencing the effectiveness of efforts to increase the economic self-reliance of refugee women fall into several major categories: the commitment of the assistance community to income-generation activities; economic and legal constraints; and planning and implementation issues.

COMMITMENT TO INCOME-GENERA-TION A major factor in the success of

African woman with sewing machine.

efforts to increase income for refugee women is the receptivity and seriousness with which donors, host country governments and project workers support these income-generating projects. While a great deal of lip-service is paid to the concept of self-help, there is little evidence of serious commitment to ensuring the long-term effectiveness of income-generating projects.

Projects for women have fallen victim to the same pressures that apply generally with regard to development approaches for refugees. UNHCR focuses its primary attention on assistance and protection for refugees, expending relatively small amounts on projects to enhance self-support. As new crises arise and funding for refugee assistance declines, donors often target their support for emergency relief. The traditional development organizations that have greater expertise in this area, the UN Development Programme, for example, lack mandates to provide ongoing support for refugee-related projects. They have not become much involved in these activities outside of special efforts such as the second International Conference on Assistance to Refugees in Africa (ICARA II). Host governments are, at best, ambivalent about these projects, fearing that the refugees may remain permanently within their borders.

Self-reliance projects for women face additional constraints. The major funding available for development-oriented projects, such as the World Bank's support of projects in Pakistan, has emphasized activities to improve the infrastructure of the host country, or large agricultural efforts. Examples of such projects are those for reforestation and road-building. Although not labelled as 'men's projects', the intended participants have generally been men, with an understanding that the projects would be implemented outside the refugee camps and require hard, manual labour.

No women have been integrated into these programmes.

Usually, women's involvement in income-generating activities has been through projects clearly defined as 'women's' programmes. There are many reasons to classify projects by gender. Most specifically, women-only projects provide a greater opportunity to address the cultural constraints on women's participation in income-generating activities. Some of the most successful projects, in terms of recruitment of participants, spent considerable time determining what were culturally appropriate ways to conduct classes or provide work space to women.

Women-specific projects provide some advantages, but as implemented they have tended to present problems as well. In most locations, the trend is to involve women in marginal economic activities because they are seen as traditional or acceptable; the universal emphasis on handicrafts and sewing projects is illustrative.

The agencies implementing projects vary greatly in their approach to income-generation. Some agencies built on previous experience with women and development programmes, and were, therefore, fully committed to economic as well as social ends; others approached the issue from a social service perspective which, combined with little experience or expertise in designing projects with economic objectives, led to minimal economic achievement.

To illustrate one approach: Save the Children Fund (SCF) views women not as a special group, but rather as the logical targets for participation in development projects. In SCF's experience, benefits from activities targeted at women extend to the entire family and to the community. Following this philosophy, in Sudan, SCF employs an integrated, multi-disciplinary assistance approach which has helped the

Beneficiary of loan to open small shop.

agency establish credibility within the refugee community. SCF uses its health-care activities to bring staff into contact with women who are appropriate targets for economic schemes. The agency employs refugee women as staff and uti-lizes a system of women home visitors as an alternative source of information gathering. Most importantly, income-generation for women was viewed not as a token activity, but one among several involving women.

ECONOMIC AND LEGAL CONSTRAINTS

Even where the commitment to increased self-reliance of refugee women is unim-peachable, projects face difficult economic constraints: many projects have been implemented in countries facing their own economic crises, with high levels of infla-tion soon rendering planning budgets obsolete; transportation costs have been high, if transportation is even available; refugee camps and settlements and the surrounding villages are often poor, pro-viding inadequate markets for project par-ticipants' products; and local unemploy-ment has made it difficult for refugees to compete with local inhabitants for scarce jobs, even if they receive appropriate training.

Beyond these economic constraints are legal ones. Refugees often do not qualify for work permits or business licences. Where these are available, the procedures for obtaining one may be long, difficult and costly. Some implementing agencies lack either the resources or will to go through these processes on behalf of par-ticipants. In addition, refugees are general-ly not allowed to own land or standing structures; they need to rent them, often at exorbitant costs, from local residents. Travel documents are a third limitation. Refugees may not receive permission to travel to markets. Legal constraints make it difficult, if not impossible, for refugee

businesses to survive. In some cases, the continued dependence on international assistance is due as much to legal, as to economic pressures. As a 'project', the income-generation activity could be imple-mented, but as an independent business it would be illegal or on a shaky legal basis. While these economic and legal limitations are very serious, some projects have addressed them more successfully than others. Setting up co-operatives has been an important factor in helping projects to succeed both in Sudan and Costa Rica, for example.

The Sudanese government allows refugee endeavours to register as official co-operatives. This gives the refugees access to goods, such as sugar, at the offi-cial price. Co-operatives can also provide a needed economic base for funding busi-ness activities. The Wad Awad co-operative is a good example. Established in 1981, this co-operative negotiated with the Sudanese Cooperative Office and the Commission on Refugees for permission to open a shop. It also obtained control over a grinding mill, received a lorry from UNHCR, and opened a welding shop. Plans are underway to provide electricity and ambulance/transport service. All these activities have been organized by the refugees, and they are legal and recog-nized as such by the government.

In Costa Rica, the limitations on the number of aliens employed by a business do not apply to co-operatives. Therefore, projects utilizing co-operative structures are not subject to the same problems in hiring refugee workers as would be other businesses in the country. Some of the planned self-sufficiency activities exam-ined for a report, prepared in 1987, for example, a fisheries project which will provide jobs for both women and men, envisioned use of co-operatives composed equally of Costa Ricans and Nicaraguans. The project planners expected to receive permission for their activities because of the legal structure chosen, as well as the involvement of host-country nationals.

Other projects have bypassed legal constraints on their implementation through direct negotiations with officials of the host government. Here, an important ingredient is trust. In one case, for example, an indigenous voluntary agency has been able to implement training programmes in camps where the official policy strongly prohibits these activities and foreign agencies have been denied permission to begin similar activities. In other cases, a particularly knowledgeable administrator has understood the loopholes in local laws and taken advantage of them for the benefit of the project.

PLANNING AND IMPLEMENTATION

Certain approaches to planning and implementation appear to have contributed to the success of income-generation projects:

- **Clearly defined objectives:** The concept of an income-generation activity can have different connotations for different individuals. While variation, in itself, is not a problem, it can lead to confusion about the basic nature and objectives of the project. Many 'income-generation' projects encompassed other worthy objectives, such as literacy or health and nutrition training. Those projects which kept income-generation as the primary goal, regardless of the nature of secondary objectives, seemed to accomplish the most benefits for participants, at least as far as income is concerned. Many income-generation projects for refugee women have been mislabelled because non-income generation projects (that is, social service projects) have been subsumed under the rubric 'income-generation' even though their economic objectives were secondary.

It appears that at a minimum, an income-generation project should be committed to the following objectives: 1) the primary goal is to generate income for the participants; 2) the income generated should be in proportion to the amount of time and energy the refugee women must invest in the activity; otherwise, time is lost for which they could have engaged in other potentially more productive activities; and 3) staff and participants must have a mutual understanding of the project's goals and outcomes. The most important factor is that refugee women and project staff have a clear understanding of why the project is being implemented. Other goals can be included in the project but, as discussed below, mechanisms such as progress evaluations are needed to keep multi-goal projects on track.

- **Knowledge of the population:** Few agencies implementing income-generation projects conducted needs assessments or obtained demographic breakdowns of the population they hoped to serve. They relied on staff perception of need and the resources that refugees would bring to the programmes. Projects differed greatly, however, in the accuracy of these judgements, with some implementing agencies having better information about their actual or potential clients than did others.

Agencies which possessed a good knowledge of the refugee population were better able to target the resources to the most needy and deserving. They were also able to build on the existing skills and interests of the refugees. Otherwise, problems developed. In several cases, agencies had assumed that the refugee women would be interested in sewing workshops. They then had difficulty recruiting participants because, in fact, the refugee women had little prior experience. Even where the projects did recruit participants, we heard from the refugees that they would not have independently chosen this activity had others been available.

Not all projects were clear about the people they were targeting to participate. A range of options is available. Projects can aim at increasing self-sufficiency for the individual, the family, the project or the settlement. Also, an agency can target the project for women only, the whole family or an integrated group. Agencies did not always examine the appropriateness of their employment strategy *vis-à-vis* their target group, however. For example, projects targeted single heads of households, required full-time participation, and then offered part-time wages that were insufficient to support a whole household. While such a strategy may have worked if aimed at the second wage earner within a family, it caused hardships for participants who then had no time to earn supplemental income.

- **Addressing cultural constraints:** A noticeable difference between agencies lay in their ability to differentiate between real versus imagined cultural constraints. Agencies with a better understanding of and rapport with the community were able more effectively to implement the programmes. They could avoid obvious problems or let the women decide whether the proposed activity would cause difficulties for them. For example, when working with Afghans in Pakistan, it is essential that women and men have separate work facilities. This requirement does not mean, however, that females and males cannot work on the same project. Some agencies implemented schemes involving both sexes but devised ways to keep

women and men workers separate where cultural dictates demanded it.

Similarly, a home gardening project in Sudan shows the need to probe for information about the precise interpretation of presumed cultural constraints. The men said that the women would not be interested in the project. The women, however, were interested and said it would not be a problem as the gardens were next to their houses. The agencies should make efforts to preserve the refugees' traditions, but simultaneously they must guard against an over-stringent interpretation of the traditions' requirements.

Another important factor is the ability of both expatriate and local staff to communicate with the refugee women. Development groups have stressed the importance of appropriate language skills not only in designing projects but also in overcoming problems and in managing disputes; this has often resulted in hiring local staff. When working with refugee women, however, expatriate staff must keep in mind that even if the local staff speak the official language of the country, it does not follow that they will be able to communicate with large numbers of refugee women; possibly only refugee staff will have the necessary communications skill.

- **A knowledge of the host country:** A good knowledge of the host country situation improves the likelihood of project success. A surprising number of projects were undertaken without a clear understanding of the host country's laws, markets, government structures, and so on. In Pakistan, for example, the Craft Design and Marketing project to produce Afghan handicrafts assumed that it could attempt to export the crafts internationally, but then discovered that

Pakistan was not willing to use its import quota into the US for these products. Another example is a brick-making co-operative in Khasm el Girba. This co-operative is by far the most successful income-generation activity in Sudan; it was not, however, a legally registered co-operative.

- **Project implementation:** Many income-generation projects for women suffer from implementation problems. Evaluations have shown that feasibility studies, in order to identify which problems would be faced, were too rarely undertaken before the project design was finalized. In some cases, the problems could have been anticipated and solved; in others, the project should have been scrapped.

Several problems seem to be common. Among the most frequently cited obstacles to effective programme implementation have been: marketing difficulties; difficulties in obtaining raw materials; quality control problems; transportation problems in getting goods to markets or, alternatively, getting workers to jobs; inadequately trained staff; lack of skills among participants; lack of monitoring and evaluation; and inappropriate funding cycles which provided too little time for projects to become operational and effective before further funding decisions were to be made.

STEPS TO BE TAKEN TO IMPROVE ECONOMIC ACTIVITIES FOR REFUGEE WOMEN

- Ensure that refugee and displaced women have equal access to programmes designed to increase economic self-sufficiency.

- Ensure the full participation of refugee and displaced women in the design and implementation of these programmes.

- Give high priority to integrating refugee and displaced women into all development plans. Projects that target women should be implemented where there are cultural or other barriers to overcome that do not equally affect men.

- Monitor projects carefully to ensure that they provide sufficient household income and do not focus on marginal economic activities.

- Provide technical assistance to agencies implementing economic projects to ensure more effective planning, implementation, monitoring and evaluation.

CONCLUSION ☐ Despite various obstacles to the involvement of refugee women in income-generating programmes, their interest and willingness to participate in such economic activities is clear. From both necessity and desire to better their lives, refugee women undertake to engage in outside employment, agricultural efforts, and other income-producing activities. Imaginative programmes are needed to help ensure their access to an important means of economic support.

---

1   UNHCR, n.d.
2   Robert Chambers, 1986.
3   Susan Forbes Martin and Emily Copeland, 1987, p. 19.
4   During 1990, there were a number of attacks on Afghan women's projects in Pakistan, putting into question the viability of these approaches as well as raising serious questions about the protection of refugee women.
5   See for example, Martin and Copeland, 1987, and Eve Hall, in Ninette Kelly, 1989.
6   Austrian Relief Committee, 1985–86.

⑥ DURABLE SOLUTIONS

A tall thin man emerges cautiously from the shadows. He walks into the glare of the headlights, and looks unbelievingly at the young woman in front of him. It is Lydia, the youngest of his nine children. 'I had heard that people were coming back,' the old man tells us. 'And when I heard the car approaching, I thought to myself, maybe it's her. Perhaps she really has come home. But I still can't believe it.' As he speaks, other members of the family, brothers, sisters, uncles and aunts, appear from the darkness, whooping with surprise and delight as they catch sight of their long-lost relative.'

A MAJOR GOAL of the refugee system is to find durable solutions for those who have been forced to flee their homes. There are three such solutions: voluntary return to one's country of origin, settlement in a country of first asylum, and resettlement in a third country. The most desirable is voluntary return to one's country of origin, hopefully after conditions have changed sufficiently to permit peaceful and safe reintegration. Refugees able to go back to their homelands already know the culture of lifestyles there, which means they can avoid the painful transitions that other refugees must face. Moreover, they often have family or community resources in place to aid them socially and economically upon their return.

Where safe return is unlikely, at least for a long time, the next best option is settlement in neighbouring countries. Such countries often share cultural values, and refugees may be able to live with ethnic

---

Table 6.1: Significant Voluntary Repatriations: 1990

Voluntary repatriation numbers reflect estimates of refugees who spontaneously returned to their homelands, as well as those people who participated in formal programs administered by UNHCR. This is not a comprehensive list, and no total is given.

To	From	Numbers
Afghanistan	Iran	36,000–60,000
Afghanistan	Pakistan	80,000–200,000
Angola	Zaire	2,200
Chad	Central African Republic	11,000
El Salvador	Honduras	8,000
Guatemala	Mexico	780
Iraq	Iran	4,500
Iraq	Turkey	2,500
Laos	Thailand	1,480
Mali	Algeria	2,000
Namibia	Angola	2,000
Nicaragua	Honduras and Costa Rica	30,100
Vietnam	Hong Kong	5,430

© United States Committee for Refugees

---

cousins; physical and economic conditions are also likely to be similar, thus reducing the need for major adjustment to new circumstances.

Repatriation and permanent settlement in a neighbouring country may not be possible for some refugees. In these cases, resettlement to a third country may be necessary both for the refugees' protection and as the only possible, durable solution to their situation. Resettlement, which presents different issues and problems for refugee women than do the other two solutions, is discussed elsewhere.

PEACE, RECONSTRUCTION AND REPATRIATION ☐ Voluntary repatriation in peace and dignity is by far the preferred solution to any refugee situation. Since World War II, that solution has been possible in a number of situations in which massive numbers of refugees have been able to return to their home countries. Following the declaration of independence in many former colonies or territories of other countries, such returns have been common. The most massive repatriation programme involved refugees returning to Bangladesh after its formation in December 1971: within four months, more than 10 million refugees returned to their homes. Other countries seeing significant returns include Angola, Burma, Guinea-Bissau, Mozambique, Nicaragua and Zimbabwe. In a number of these situations, however, the peace that brought return was short-lived and further displacements occurred in subsequent years.

It is generally assumed that refugee women will be a force for voluntary return if given the opportunity; anecdotal information lends support to this idea. Cambodian, Afghan and Mozambican

women have spoken to Western women of their desire to return home. They hope to see their parents before it is too late. They also tell of aspirations for their children, which revolve around return and reconstruction of their home countries. They speak as well of their fear that their children and their children's children will never see the home country again.[2]

Refugee women also express their anxieties about return. As one report notes, 'They are longing for their home country but their first condition for going back is that there must be peace.'[3]

While the wars, repression and poor economic conditions which displaced millions of people still persist, repatriation has become reality for many and a realistic hope for others. Peace and/or democratization have become realities in a number of places, for example, Namibia, Nicaragua, Iran, Eastern Europe, and

African woman repatriating to Namibia.

foreign troops have been withdrawn from a number of conflict areas, such as Afghanistan. Peace talks are underway in countries with longstanding civil conflicts, including Angola, El Salvador, and Cambodia. Finally, the discussions between the South African government and the African National Congress have prompted plans for repatriation of many of that country's displaced people.

Even with these promising international developments, repatriation is not an easily achieved solution for refugees. In several of these countries, conflicts involving external military forces have given way to internal conflicts that are no less bloody than those that forced the refugees into exile; that is certainly the situation in Afghanistan. Even when peace comes, the problems of reconstruction are formidable. In many developing countries the conflicts that have caused so many to seek refuge elsewhere have also been responsible for destroying the economy and much of the infrastructure.

The home countries, for their part, may be ambivalent about the return of their citizens. On the one hand, the people's willingness to return is a potent symbol of a new government's legitimacy, particularly one striving to show that it has established democratic institutions. On the other hand, many developing countries lack adequate economic resources to reintegrate their citizens, that is, to provide jobs, housing, medical care, food, and so on. Citizens who have remained in their country through the fall of one regime and the emergence of a new one may be antagonistic towards the prospect of expending scarce resources to assist those who fled. It may even be seen to be in the interest of those who remained for the exiles to stay abroad. For example, remittances from migrants who have gone to industrial countries provide an important source of economic support regardless of the reasons for migration.

Because of the economic gulf that often exists between country of asylum and country of repatriation, return from industrialized countries is particularly problematic. Repatriation is clearly the goal of many refugees and displaced persons who have settled in industrialized countries as it is for those who have been in developing ones. It is not unusual for such migrants to proclaim their intentions to return to their homelands as soon as the violence abates and/or repressive governments are replaced. Yet, the road from hope to realization is often difficult for those who have been settled in Europe and North America, particularly when they have become integrated socially and economically.

If and when voluntary return takes place, the assistance needs of the returnees will be great. Beatrice Manz has written about repatriation of Guatemalan refugees:

For any repatriation to be successful, the refugees need to regain their economic means of survival, which means regaining their land and reintegration into the local economies. They will need economic aid to farm that land and assistance must be guaranteed until the refugees have achieved self-sufficiency.[4]

A number of factors will influence planning for potential repatriation, including development programmes aimed at assisting refugees to reintegrate.

- *The scope and scale of repatriation efforts:* These programmes differ in, for example: size of the refugee population; the period of time during which repatriation takes place; the number of places from and to which the refugees move; the number of organizations providing assistance; and the amount of funding available for assistance programmes.

- *Contexts in which repatriation takes place:* Repatriation programmes differ according to the conditions to which the refugees will return. In some situations, relative peace may have been secured prior to any return, in others, continued fighting and targeted repression is likely. Understanding the relationship between refugees and resistance forces is also necessary to understanding the outcome of repatriation programmes in some locations.

- *Assistance to returnees:* Thorough needs assessments must be conducted to determine what types of assistance will be needed by returnees; what agencies should be involved in providing assistance (intergovernmental organizations, the country of return, non-governmental agencies, other governments through bilateral contributions, and so on); what, if any, co-ordination will be needed; and which agency should provide it.

- *Relationship between refugee assistance and reconstruction efforts:* Repatriation programmes cannot be implemented in a vacuum because they are an essential part of the process of reconstructing the home country. Early decisions on how best to co-ordinate assistance to refugees and efforts to reconstruct the country are therefore essential.

- *Protection of returnees:* Some repatriations take place without a guarantee of safety, but it is preferable to know what provisions are in place for ensuring the protection of returnees before their repatriation. Provisions are also needed to ensure the voluntary nature of repatriation. And the problem of protection against probable dangers, for example, the presence of land mines in conflict zones, must be identified and steps taken to address them.

- *Additional population movements:* Return

of refugees may be only one part of an exchange of population following significant changes in a country's political life. It is necessary to understand the movement patterns of those who had been internally displaced within the borders of the country; out-migration of those who are on the losing side of any settlement; migration of people in jeopardy due to continued fighting; and migration to neighbouring countries of those unable to support themselves in economic terms in the home country.

- *The needs and potentialities of sub-populations of returnees:* As in other aspects of refugee programming, repatriation has differential impacts depending on the gender and age of returnees. Specific issues pertaining to women and children must be identified and plans made to address their needs and help them participate fully in the repatriation process.

REPATRIATION AND THE PROTECTION OF WOMEN
The Note on Refugee Women and International Protection submitted to the forty-first session of the UNHCR Executive Committee reports that:

Generally speaking, there is relatively little information available regarding the international protection concerns that are specific to refugee women in relation to durable solutions. On the other hand, while further study is therefore recommended, some issues are sufficiently documented to warrant being addressed.

Many of the physical protection issues facing refugee women and children in flight hold similar potential on return, particularly where return is spontaneous and unassisted. Women and children may be subject to the same type of physical and sexual abuse from border guards, for example, in crossing the border back to their home country. Internally displaced persons may face similar problems in returning to their home villages.

Once back, the returnees may experience harassment, or more serious problems related to their protection, from the authorities and/or villagers who remained at home. Issues of land ownership, for example, may generate tensions resulting in violence. Where male family members have been killed, women returnees may face special problems in reclaiming their property.

While some repatriations occur after a peace settlement has been implemented, others take place during periods of continuing hostilities. Moreover, the government that initiated actions against the refugees, and thereby led to their flight, may still be in power.

Where responsibility for the protection of returnees lies is often unclear. Since individuals are again within their own country, their government should have the principal protection function. Yet return often occurs under circumstances in which the good will of the government cannot be assumed. The role of international organizations is likely to be limited, however, and subject to the government's willingness to permit their presence. NGOs also require permission of the countries of origin, but their presence may be desired if they are able to bring resources with them. By their very presence, NGOs often play an important protection role because they are the only outsiders able to monitor possible abuses.

A further protection problem involves the actual decision to return. Such decisions are frequently made by camp leaders (usually men) and there may be little opportunity for women to express their views either as a group or as individuals. This can cut two ways. In some situations, women who would like to return to their homes are prevented from doing so

because male leaders have determined that no one should return. Along the Thai–Cambodian border, for example, many women and children are in effect captives of the resistance groups that control the camps. Conversely, women may be compelled to return 'voluntarily' because of reductions in assistance, poor living conditions, and physical abuse. A delegation examining the situation of Vietnamese women and children in Hong Kong reported:

It appears from our discussions with women who have chosen to return that some Vietnamese are being coerced into doing so under the guise of 'voluntary repatriation'. Most of those agreeing to voluntary return have done so before undergoing screening [to determine if they meet refugee criteria], often citing the horrendous conditions in Hong Kong as their reason for volunteering to return.[5]

To complicate matters, women are not always given the information needed in order to make an informed choice. The same delegation to Hong Kong commented: 'In general, there is insufficient counselling for those asked to make as serious a decision as voluntary repatriation.... The Vietnamese have many questions about the fate that awaits them but little information about the experiences of those who preceded them.'[6]

REPATRIATION, RECONSTRUCTION AND ASSISTANCE FOR WOMEN A range of assistance issues is related to repatriation of women. The infrastructures of countries that produce refugees are often destroyed during the wars and violence that cause the movements. Refugees (and internally displaced persons) may return to villages that have no health clinics, roads, schools, food stores or other basic services. It may be months or years before

the communities become self-sustaining. During this period, most of the assistance issues, access to food, health care, education and employment (already discussed in the context of refugee movements), continue to be problems. In addition, a range of legal difficulties will need to be resolved, for example, the ownership of land formerly occupied by refugees but now inhabited by others.

The demographics of both the refugee population and the country of origin will influence the ease with which reintegration can be accomplished. For example, the demographic changes that took place in Afghanistan as a result of more than a decade of fighting will present major problems and issues for returning women. According to Nancy Hatch Dupree, a scholar of Afghan society:

Possibly nearly a million men have been killed or disabled in the *Jihad* although accurate figures are impossible to obtain. There are tens of thousands of widows with their children among the refugees; thousands of young girls have lost their intended mates; other thousands have suddenly become sole supporters of their households because their husbands are totally disabled.[7]

Having received international assistance while in refugee camps, the future of these women inside Afghanistan is not clear. Mrs Dupree goes on:

tradition...dictates that these women be provided for as enjoined in the Quran (S.4:36).... No one has yet suggested any practical means for accomplishing this. Recent tentative discussions have only just begun to identify some of the social problems which will accompany the economic responsibilities of caring for so many unattached women with their numerous children.[8]

The presence of a disproportionate number of widows in the Cambodian border camps will complicate return for that group too. In a Ford Foundation-funded demographic study of the residents of the three major encampments on the Thai–Cambodian border, about 20 per cent of the respondents were widowed. These figures correspond to the proportion of households headed by widows inside rural Cambodia as well. As with the rest of the border population, the majority of the widows on the border came from rural, farming backgrounds and assumed they would return to farming if repatriated. The report points out:

Returning to an uncertain future in Cambodia without the support of an adult male family member, lacking any material resources, and accompanied by several dependent children, would obviously be a particularly difficult experience for these women. Nor is it clear whether they could expect to locate other family members in Cambodia to provide assistance.... Tracing efforts on behalf of this group should perhaps be given priority, in view of their situation.[9]

A survey of Afghan women in Baluchistan showed that almost all women reported that basic needs, food and shelter, will be the biggest problems when they are back home; they expected the problems to be most serious in the beginning. Other problems cited were lack of money and difficulties for the men in finding jobs. Lack of health care facilities, shortage of water and landlessness were also mentioned: 'Before the war we had nothing in Afghanistan. Now it will be worse,'[10] one woman stated.

A survey, prepared for UNICEF, of trained Afghan women in Pakistan identified a number of priorites for repatriation.[11] These included:

- **Education:** About 70 per cent of the women surveyed cited education as a top priority in the reconstruction of Afghanistan. They noted that reconstruction would not be effective if the populace were uneducated. The two most critical needs regarding education were teacher training and expansion of female education.

- **Health care:** The women supposed that health care, poor prior to the Soviet invasion, had deteriorated as a result of ten years of war. They noted that the rigours of the return as well as landmine explosions and inter-group conflicts were likely to produce an increased need for health care. Further, they stated that the refugees had become accustomed to a higher level of health care in Pakistan and therefore would have heightened expectations. The educated women argued that it would be wise to take advantage of this situation in order that people, especially women, become more and more accustomed to seeking health assistance when needed.

- **Future of widows, women with handicapped husbands, and orphans:** The traditional social welfare system which existed in Afghanistan had broken down, the women stated. Traditionally, widows were absorbed into the husband's family, sometimes marrying a brother of the husband. In current Afghanistan, however, there would be too many widows for these traditional patterns to work. Many families consist only of women and children. The widows will therefore require special programmes including a registration process to identify widows among the refugees, assistance in returning to their homes, assistance in rebuilding their homes, and training programmes to prepare them to earn money to support their families.

Similar issues can be found regarding Cambodian repatriation. For example, only 13 per cent of the population inside Cambodia has access to safe drinking water; sanitation and street drainage are also poor.[12] The returnees, having lived in camps reliant on trucked-in water for years, will not have immunity against many of the diseases found in the water. Women, as the principal water carriers, will be particularly prone to water-borne diseases, as has already been noted.

Cambodia also suffers from a lack of trained medical personnel. Few Cambodian physicians, nurses or other health workers survived the Khmer Rouge years. During the past year, many Eastern European physicians and nurses who helped run the limited health facilities in Cambodia have returned to their own countries. In addition, many hospitals and clinics were destroyed either during the reign of the Khmer Rouge or as a result of the fighting of the past decade. While remarkable efforts have been made to train health personnel and build the physical infrastructure, health resources are still inadequate. Hospitals and clinics lack drugs and equipment as well as 'basic necessities such as electricity, lighting, clean water, sewage and garbage disposal and proper sterilization and laundry facilities'.[13]

Women will face potential economic problems on their return to Cambodia. The productive capacity of Cambodia's economy remains far below the levels attained in the 1960s, prior to decades of conflict. Per capita income was estimated to be US$60 in 1988.[14] Many of the displaced population come from rural areas and will be returning to agricultural life. Women, traditionally, have played an important role in agriculture. For example, they are responsible for most of the sowing, transplanting and harvesting of rice, the staple crop. Most Cambodians at the

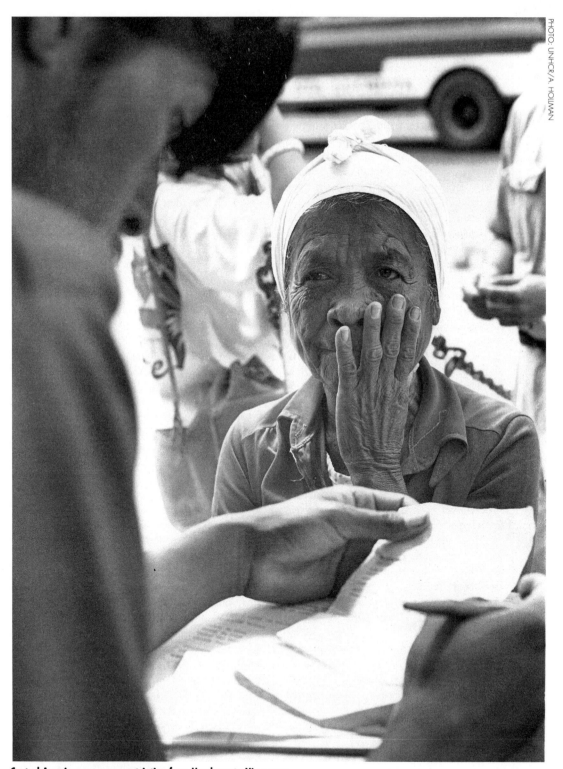

Central American woman repatriating from Honduras to Nicaragua.

border expect to return to farming, but those born in the camps or who were young children when they came to the border have never experienced farming work. The UNICEF report on Cambodia confirms that 'women farming on their own are at a particular disadvantage because [of] the traditional labour exchange system [between men and women]'.[15]

A major issue facing those planning repatriation is how to utilize the talents to be found in the refugee camps to help in the reconstruction of the countries of origin. Tapping the resources that women bring to bear in development will be essential to this process. Because the skewed demographics (owing to war casualties) of the refugee population are also to be found among the population that remained, a high proportion of those involved overall in reconstruction will be women.

The survey on Afghan returnees prepared for UNICEF, cited above, demonstrated the diversity of resources that women will bring to repatriation but it also showed serious obstacles to their active involvement in reconstruction. The survey sought to identify women in refugee villages and urban areas who have received training in education and health fields, to evaluate the role they may play in repatriation and reconstruction, and to make recommendations on the kinds of programmes that should be funded to assist in rebuilding Afghanistan.

The survey found that the proportion of Afghan women who had been trained prior to coming to Pakistan was minimal. A larger number of women had received training through refugee programmes as health workers and traditional birth attendants. Many of these women had, however, received only superficial instruction in basic mother/child health care. Only about 5 per cent of the women identified during the survey had received training which could be considered adequate by international standards. Most were teachers, with a smaller number being trained medical personnel.

The survey noted an interest on the part of NGOs to upgrade their skills-training programmes for refugee women. But it appeared that the NGOs were not adequately prepared to take on this role; they would need help in designing programmes. The authors of the survey recommended that the most skilled women be chosen to serve as trainers, networkers and supervisors in order to facilitate the dissemination of their expertise throughout the community.[16]

There were several obstacles militating against fully utilizing these skilled women's resources. Many of them were committed to using their skills but expressed concern about returning to Afghanistan, particularly if a fundamentalist government were installed. One woman noted: 'Our most serious problem will be overcoming the narrow-mindedness of men who want to keep the women at home and will use the Russian invasion as their justification.'[17]

According to the survey, the trained women tended to come from only two areas inside Afghanistan, namely Kabul and Kandahar. Most wanted to return to their former places of residence although a small number indicated a willingness to go wherever their skills were needed. The latter wanted to organize educated women to supervise outreach programmes for rural women. One of the side benefits of the refugee situation, it appeared, was to sensitize educated, urban Afghan women to the needs of the rural women. As one woman stated:

I never realized how bad the situation for rural women was until I walked out

Mexican Guatemalan refugees.

through the countryside and then worked with women in the refugee villages. It now will be up to the educated women to do something for their rural sisters. Those of us who have medical training are particularly responsible to help them learn to take care of themselves and their children.[18]

At the urgings of educated women associated with all the political parties, a women's centre was established in Peshawar to serve as an assembly point for women concerned about repatriation. In addition, the centre provided skills-training and literacy programmes for Afghan women in order to help the productiveness of a larger cross-section of women on return.

The reintegration of skilled and professional refugee women has proved difficult in a number of repatriations. One scientist who returned to her home country explained some of the difficulties: 'Lack of stability in the country, lack of stability on the job, lack of fair and nondiscriminatory guidelines for appointments and promotions, lack of social insertion, poor salaries and working conditions, lack of positions due to frozen science budgets and to the consolidation of stagnated facilities.' Resentment of colleagues who remained behind is one of the most difficult issues to deal with in returning:

The returning scientists will be accused of desertion, of not having gone through the pains endured by their counterparts who stayed behind. The reasons of their leaving — even when forced — will be neglected in favor of self-pitying remarks on personal hardships — even when exile itself was a hardship.[19]

The UNICEF study of the skills of Afghan women noted that programmes should be established to sensitize male refugees to the need to involve women in repatriation and reconstruction:

During the Inventory process, quite a few supportive men were encountered, including high level resistance party officials. These men have begun to realize that the support of women will be important because of the large number of men who have died, been seriously maimed, or will not return to Afghanistan.... Supportive men should be involved in developing and implementing these... sensitization programmes because, after all, most of them undoubtedly went through the process themselves.[20]

STEPS TO BE TAKEN TO ENHANCE THE RETURN OF WOMEN IN PEACE AND DIGNITY

- Analyse the protection and assistance needs of refugee women and children upon repatriation. Such analysis is urgently needed, given the potential for repatriation of millions of refugees. Country-specific assessments should be conducted, as well as a synthesis of information in order to determine what changes are needed in planning for future repatriations.

- Ensure that women who want to return are able to do so and that those fearing return are provided protection against forced repatriation.

- Integrate women fully into development projects designed to ease the reintegration of refugees into their home countries.

The results of the survey further pointed to the need to think through the requirements of repatriation, from the women's point of view, at the beginning rather than the end of a refugee experience. The study included a number of recommendations for training programmes which, had they been in operation for ten years, would have provided a good base of trained refugee women to help with repatriation and reconstruction.

A mission that examined the situation of women who had returned to Namibia reiterated the need to take such situations into account through all stages of planning for repatriation:

'... the situation underlined the need to plan with the needs of returnee women in mind, not as a separate category and certainly not as an afterthought, but as an integral part of the overall planning for the returnees. Including them at every stage of the planning process is essential to ensure that there will be no suprises along the way.[21]

SETTLEMENT IN COUNTRIES OF ASYLUM

☐ In a number of countries, particularly in Africa, refugees have been permitted to remain indefinitely in the country in which they initially sought asylum. Some move into rural settlements; others settle spontaneously in cities. For a period of time, the settled refugees are generally provided with international assistance to help them adjust and to minimize their impact on the host countries. Significant local settlement has been seen in Sudan, Tanzania, Zaire, Costa Rica, Mexico, and elsewhere.

In rural settlements, many of the assistance issues encountered in camps and upon repatriation also face refugee women and children. Access to schooling and health care are of particular concern, especially after the settlement has ceased to receive international assistance. The refugees may then be reliant on the health care and educational systems of their host country. Refugees in general, and women in particular, may be considered a low priority for provision of these services.

The decision to move refugees into settlements can be controversial too. In a number of countries, refugees have wished

Integration. African women tilling land.

to remain in border areas, closer to their home country but the host government has wanted to move them to an interior location, often for security or other reasons. At times, UNHCR has also wished to move camps, particularly where the safety of the refugees is in question at a border location. Ensuring the participation of refugee women in the decisions about moving into settlements is critical in these situations.

Legal rights are also of concern. A study of rural settlements in Africa found that few refugees were accorded full legal and political rights, even those born in the settlement. In effect, the residents remained refugees in their new homes. Without these rights, they had no capacity to influence political decisions that affected them. Absence of full legal rights also impeded their ability to attain full economic self-support because they could be denied access to markets, ownership of land and businesses, right to travel freely throughout the country, and so on. Access to employment and income support for needy families is a further issue affecting those refugee women settled in countries of asylum.

Spontaneously settled refugees, particularly those living in urban settings, face even further difficulties. Obtaining legal residency is often impossible, particularly where governments are trying to discourage settlement in cities. Even in rural areas, spontaneously settled refugees often do not have identity cards, thereby limiting their access to services.

The settlement of refugees in countries of asylum also has an impact on the residents of the host country. Often, it is the poorest residents who are most adversely affected. As one report notes, 'poorer hosts can lose from competition for food, work, wages, services and common property resources. Vulnerable hosts ... lack refugees' option of sending their weaker dependants to camps and settlements'.[22] Women and children are often the most vulnerable populations in developing countries, therefore they may suffer the greatest disadvantage from the presence of refugees. This issue needs much more attention from those planning assistance programmes in refugee situations.

STEPS TO FACILITATE LONGER-TERM INTEGRATION AND DEVELOPMENT

- Ensure that refugee women are fully integrated into development projects designed to ease the settlement of refugees in host countries.

- Assess the impact of refugees and displaced persons on the more vulnerable persons in the surrounding populations and take actions needed to ensure that they benefit from development programmes designed to increase the integration of refugees.

- Assess the rights of settled refugee women and take actions needed to increase their legal standing.

FROM RELIEF AND DEPENDENCY TO DEVELOPMENT: WOMEN'S ROLE □

Development is emerging as a key option for dealing with the consequences of refugee movements, for the refugees themselves, the countries in which they seek safety, and their countries of origin. Recognizing that long-term care and maintenance is costly both in human and economic terms, there has been interest in exploring new, development-oriented programmes for refugees. With the aim of enhancing the economic independence of refugees in camps and local settlements, as well as easing the burden of refugees on their host country and facilitating return where possible, these programmes may be either focused exclusively on refugee participants or they may serve refugees and other residents.

Development-oriented projects have taken two major forms. First are small-scale projects that address a variety of refugee needs, such as health care, employment and education, with particular attention to enhancing the refugees' capacity for economic self-support. The second are large-scale projects to improve the host country's infrastructure.

To be successful, the development orientation must be put in place at the outset of a refugee emergency in order to guard against dependency. This approach, however, tends to run counter to the immediate demands of the crisis, when most organizations are preoccupied with saving lives. In their book on refugee aid and development, Mary Anderson and Peter Woodrow state some principles of assistance:

Both relief and development programmes should be more concerned with increasing local capacities and reducing vulnerabilities than with providing goods, services, or technical assistance. In fact, goods, services or technical assistance should be provided only insofar as they support sustainable development by increasing local capacities and reducing local vulnerabilities.

The way that such resources are transferred must be held to the same test. Programming must not be solely preoccupied with meeting urgent physical/material needs, but must integrate such needs into efforts that address the social/organizational and motivational/attitudinal elements of the situation as well.[23]

Development-oriented programmes for refugees are believed to have two major advantages:

- There is a perception that these programmes will facilitate durable solutions.

With greater capacity to provide for themselves, the refugees will be better prepared to return to their countries of origin if conditions permit, or integrate into the local society if settlement in the country of first asylum or a third country is possible.

- It is hoped that the programmes will reduce costs. A large part of the funds used in such programmes supports basic care and maintenance, including shelter, food and clothing. To the extent that refugees are able to integrate into the host country, the cost to the international community will be minimized.

There are impediments to accomplishing the development goals of refugee assistance. First, many asylum countries are concerned that development-oriented refugee assistance projects will, in fact, result in the *de facto* integration of refugees into the local society. There is concern that greater independence on the part of refugees may reduce international pressure on the country of origin for voluntary repatriation or on donor countries for contributions to the assistance system. Refugee camps are a reminder to the world community to work towards long-term solutions and to maintain their share of the burden of assisting refugees.

Second, refugees often settle in the poorest areas of their host countries, where local inhabitants also struggle to survive. To complicate matters, sufficient arable land, water, and work opportunities for both the local population and the refugees may be in short supply. In such situations, it is not possible to assist refugees without providing similar opportunities for the local inhabitants. Without satisfactory support for their own citizens, the reluctance of host governments to permit refugee development-oriented activities is to be expected.

Host countries often put two conditions on development-oriented assistance: 1) equitable burden-sharing between the international community and the host country; and 2) the provision of additional assistance to refugees. By equitable burden-sharing, the host countries mean not only direct assistance to refugees by the international community but also help to the host country in dealing with the negative impacts arising from the presence of the refugees. In this regard, the host country may request help in dealing with impacts on their infrastructure, such as the medical care system, roads, water systems and so on. A 1983 report of a Meeting of Experts on Refugee Aid and Development, convened by the UN High Commissioner for Refugees, noted:

Host countries and their populations are increasingly affected by large influxes of refugees.... Economies and services [are] under severe pressure...their own people seriously deprived.... [Refugees] place additional burden on economic and social infrastructures as well as on government administration, and may damage or destroy the environment.[24]

The presence of spontaneously settled refugees is of particular concern to host countries. Assistance from the UN system generally goes to refugee camps or settlements where refugees are registered for receiving aid, but spontaneously settled refugees generally do not present themselves for such assistance, living off the local economy instead. Thus, where there are significant numbers of the latter, it is particularly important to include both refugees and local inhabitants in development programmes.

This point leads naturally to the second issue raised by host countries: additional refugee development assistance. Host countries generally insist that refugee assistance be over and above the normal development assistance they would receive if there were no refugees in the country. Host countries, in view of their limited resources, feel it is inequitable to have to share their development aid with refugees or to incur debt on their behalf. Donors, on the other hand, point to the limited availability of development funds and to the advantages that accrue to host countries from integrating refugees into their regular development plans: refugees can then contribute to the development of the areas in which they live.

Even where the institutional and financial constraints are overcome, still other factors may influence the potential success of development-oriented approaches to refugee assistance: the state of the local economy; the skill level and educational background of the refugees; their attitude towards integrating into the host country; and the existence of viable programme ideas.

A further factor that has complicated efforts to promote development is the demographic composition of the refugee population. As discussed earlier (pp. 52–59), many of the projects designed to promote development have been geared towards men. But women and children make up the majority of the world's refugee population, therefore failure to take into account these demographic facts can adversely affect the success of development efforts. Conversely, women are an important resource for development and can make a significant contribution to building self-reliance for their communities. New approaches and new institutional arrangements may well be needed if their contributions are to be recognized and effective.

Incorporating refugee populations into development projects requires that institutions that traditionally have had responsibility for development programmes take on new roles *vis-à-vis* refugees. Until recently, almost all international assistance to refugees was administered through the UNHCR. With the new focus on development, however, development oriented organizations such as the UNDP, the World Bank, and the International Monetary Fund are also becoming involved. Private organizations with expertise and experience in implementing projects on women and development will also need to play a more active role in refugee programmes if these efforts are to be successful.

CONCLUSION ☐ Finding durable solutions to refugee situations is a major challenge for the international community. The consequences of failure to find these solutions are considerable for the refugees, the host country, the country of origin, and the international community itself. Successful solutions require that refugee women must be an integral part of all efforts.

1 Tessa Williams and Jeff Crisp, in *Refugees*, Vol. 79, 1989, p. 24.
2 Reported, for example, by delegations of the Women's Commission for Refugee Women and Children to the Thai–Cambodian border, Malawi and Pakistan.
3 Gunillio Wingo, 1990, p. 4.
4 Beatrice Manz, 1987.
5 Women's Commission for Refugee Women and Children, 1990, p. 22
6 Ibid.
7 Nancy Hatch Dupree, nd, pp. 23–4.
8 Ibid.
9 James F. Lynch, 1989.
10 Gunillio Wingo, 1990, p. 22.
11 Kerry M. Connor, 1988.
12 UNICEF, 1990, pp. 102–7.
13 Ibid., p. 64.
14 Ibid., p. 17.
15 Ibid., p. 115.
16 Kerry M. Connor, 1988, p. 5
17 Ibid., p. 31.
18 Ibid., p. 26.
19 Cora Sadosky, in *Scientists in Exile*, 1988, pp. 8–16.
20 Kerry M. Connor, 1988, pp. 39–40.
21 World YWCA, 1989.
22 Robert Chambers, in *International Migration Review*, Vol. 20, No. 2, 1986, p. 245.
23 Mary Anderson and Peter Woodrow, 1989, p. 97.
24 UNHCR, 1983 (contains report of the meeting of experts).

7 LIFE IN INDUSTRIALIZED COUNTRIES

I became a citizen last year; I am now an American.... For some refugees, becoming an American is not an easy thing to do. It means giving up that final thing that is yours, your nationality.... When I took my oath, I thought, 'Oh my God! Everything is gone!' But after it happened, I never thought about it. The most painful part was just thinking about it. There is something exciting about holding my new blue passport and knowing that I will vote next year for the president.[1]

REFUGEE WOMEN who arrive in industrialized countries are either: 1) resettled from countries of first asylum, entering through formal admission programmes; or 2) direct arrivals who come spontaneously and then request asylum.

Resettlement in third countries is generally considered to be the least desirable solution for refugees because it moves them far from their own countries and cultures. In many situations, however, resettlement is necessary in order to provide protection or durable solutions for refugees. Their country of asylum may be unwilling or unable to allow them to remain indefinitely; return to their country of origin may be impossible for the foreseeable future.

Refugees come directly to industrialized countries for a variety of reasons. Escape to North America or Europe may be easier, less dangerous and more direct for some, for example, via airplanes, than is flight to a neighbouring country. The refugees may be unwilling or unable to wait in countries of first asylum, afraid for themselves or their families. They may have spouses or other relatives, already in the industrialized country, whom they are seeking to join more quickly than the formal admissions' programmes allow. Or, their family members may not have a status in the industrialized country that permits them to reunify through regular channels with their relatives still in the country of origin. The legal processes and problems women encounter in applying for asylum are discussed in Chapter 3.

In 1989, more than 200,000 persons resettled or received asylum in industrialized countries. About one-half went to the United States; Canada and Australia accounted for 45,000; the remainder went to Europe, with France, Germany and Sweden accounting for the largest proportion.

Most of the refugee women and children who are resettled in third countries entered as part of a complete family unit. Among some refugee populations, however, a significant number of women-headed households have been resettled. Special efforts have been made to find resettlement opportunities for women who are particularly at risk in countries of first asylum. These include single women, as well as victims of piracy, rape and torture.

All refugees in industrialized countries, regardless of their family composition, face adjustment problems. These problems can be particularly acute when the cultures of the home country and the new country are markedly different. Most resettled refugees need to learn a new language, find and maintain employment, often being exposed for the first time to industrial economies, as well as adapt to life in urban settings, a difficult process for those who have lived only in rural areas before resettlement.

For refugee women, such adjustments may be particularly difficult. Yet resettled

Table 7.1: Refugees resettled and persons granted asylum in relationship to indigenous populations

Top 14 Countries (in order of refugees-to-population ratio)

RESETTLEMENT COUNTRY	1975–1989 Cumulative	1989 Only	Population in millions	Ratio Refugees/ Population
Sweden	108,315	23,961	8.5	1/78
Canada	287,225	35,000	26.6	1/93
Australia	172,823	11,663	17.1	1/99
Denmark	28,733	N/A	5.1	1/177
United States	1,355,858°	106,250	251.4	1/185
Norway	17,941	7,450	4.2	1/234
New Zealand	10,988	802	3.3	1/300
France	186,957	8,711	56.4	1/302
Switzerland	21,487	821	6.7	1/312
Austria	20,571	2,070	7.6	1/369
Netherlands	20,171	2,755	14.9	1/739
Germany (FRG)	84,960	5,991+	63.2	1/744
Spain	38,186	3,677	39.4	1/1,032
United Kingdom	13,797°	1,587	57.4	1/4,160

© United States Committee for Refugees

NOTE: The primary source for numbers of refugees resettled or granted asylum was the US State Department. Countries that have established resettlement programs generally provide particularly precise data, but data were not available for all countries for all years.

° Denotes that statistics were unavailable for 1975–81.

+ Does not include 720,000 ethnic Germans from GDR, USSR, and Eastern Europe.

women have also shown themselves to be strong resources for the development of their own ethnic communities and their new societies. This chapter explores both the needs and opportunities that the re-settlement of refugee women provides.

ADMISSION ☐ As already noted, refugee women go to industrialized countries either through resettlement programmes or as asylum seekers. Both routes are subject to pitfalls. Asylum seekers generally enter without prior approval of the new country, which must then determine whether or not the asylum seeker can remain and in what capacity. Signatories to the 1951 UN Convention Relating to the Status of Refugees agree that they will not deport refugees to a country where their life or liberty would be threatened. A grant of asylum does not necessarily mean, however, that the individual will be able to stay permanently in that country. A first step towards being granted permanent refuge, however, is to demonstrate that one meets the refugee definition. Chapter 3 examined the problems faced by refugee women during the refugee-determination process.

Resettlement decisions are made by

governments, often in consultation with UNHCR. Governments are under no obligation to take in refugees from abroad, but have complete discretion in determining whether or not they will accept refugees for resettlement. A number of countries, however, including the United States, Canada, Australia, New Zealand and most European countries, offer resettlement quotas on a yearly basis.

Typically, governments set admission levels and priorities at the start of the year. Most countries establish family reunification as a key purpose of their refugee resettlement and immigration programmes. In addition, governments offer resettlement to individuals who are of special concern, either to those who have a close personal relationship to the resettlement country (for example, having worked for one of their institutions or having gone to school there) and/or to individuals from countries in which the resettlement country has a special interest (for example, a former colony or ally in a conflict). Finally, resettlement slots are often provided to refugees who would otherwise be returned to their countries of origin or whose protection is otherwise dependent on resettlement. Several countries also run specialized programmes for individuals with particular needs: disabled; unaccompanied minors; and, as discussed below, women at risk.

Applicants for resettlement generally must demonstrate that they are refugees under international and/or national law. In addition, they are required to meet other admissions standards; for example, they may need to demonstrate that they are likely to be able to adjust to the new culture. Considerations taken into account include: knowledge of the resettlement country's language; skill levels; family members already in the resettlement coun-

try; and willingness of the government concerned or private agencies or groups to sponsor the new arrival.

Among the refugees that UNHCR believes are in desperate need of resettlement are women who do not otherwise fit the resettlement countries' criteria for admission. These women have generally experienced severe trauma and are living in circumstances in which their traditional support systems have broken down. Yet, they may have no relatives in a third country, no knowledge of the language or transferable skills, and may demonstrate a level of need that makes private groups unwilling to risk sponsorship, which requires a financial commitment.

In response to the difficulties faced by such women UNHCR has requested that countries establish a special programme for their admission or introduce a process within the normal refugee programme to permit additional admissions to cover this need. UNHCR identifies women at risk who are in need of resettlement and requests spaces from resettlement countries. To date, three countries have established programmes: Canada, Australia and New Zealand. Several other countries grant resettlement to these refugee women under the normal processing modalities. UNHCR also encourages special programmes that address some of the special needs women at risk may have to help the resettled women adjust to their new lives.

Canada's programme has been operating the longest and provides the clearest picture of the elements of the special provisions. The guidelines of the programme specify 'certain relaxation in admissibility criteria', stating that 'the greater the need for protection, the lower the threshold which the applicant should have to meet in terms of potential for successful establishment in Canada'.

**Women of first priority were those
identified overseas as having specific
protection needs in refugee camps, were
being harassed by local authorities
outside their country, or were in danger
of being returned (*refouled*) to their
home country. Of second priority were
women not in 'immediate peril' but
whose low skills level, dependent
children and other factors meant that
they had been passed over by Canada or
by other resettlement countries in the
past.[2]**

Between November 1988 and May 1990,
194 persons arrived under the Women-at-
Risk programme in Canada; they included
78 women and 116 dependants, who were
dispersed across Canada, with the majority
in British Columbia and Ontario. The
largest numbers came from Ethiopia (25
cases), Vietnam (23) and Iran (8).
Australia's Women-at-Risk programme is
prepared to offer places to 60 cases, and
New Zealand's programme is set at 20
cases. These numbers, assuming that
Canada will maintain its current pace,
account for about half of the 880 people
that UNHCR has estimated as being in
need of resettlement in 1991.[3]

NEEDS ☐ Refugee women who are
resettled in industrialized nations do
not conform to a single profile. They
come from a variety of countries, and
have had different educational and
employment experiences. The majority
originally lived in developing countries,
particularly Vietnam, Cambodia, Laos, El
Salvador, Iran, Ethiopia, Chile and Cuba.
Some, however, are from other industrialized societies, primarily Eastern Europe
and the Soviet Union. On arrival, few are
familiar with the language or customs of
the new country. A minority, however,
enters with substantial previous education
and skills.

Adjustment to the new culture can be
difficult. Barriers to successful adjustment
include those within the host society as
well as individual or personal ones.
Among the former are racial intolerance
and sexual and cultural discrimination.
Many refugees are of a different race from
the majority of the population of their new
country. As women, they may face the
dual problem of racism and sexism in
seeking employment, training or otherwise
participating in the new country's activities.

A further societal factor in adjustment is
legal status, an important factor influencing the ease with which she (or he) will be
able to adjust. Refugees who have been
resettled from overseas are legally in the
country upon arrival and generally enjoy
all legal rights of other residents. Asylum
seekers are generally in a more insecure
position while they await their hearings:
they may be ineligible to seek employment
or receive services; the procedure may be
protracted, leaving them in limbo for long
periods of time. Not knowing if they will
be able to remain permanently, asylum
seekers may not actively seek out adjustment services.

Personal barriers include family conflicts, traumas suffered during flight, illiteracy, lack of language skills, and religious
constraints. Changes in family roles often
accompany resettlement; some families
have experienced long periods of separation. Male roles may change drastically in
the new society. If their skills are not readily transferable to industrialized countries
(for example, agricultural skills), the men
may find themselves unable to support
their families:

**Men often feel neglected and disappointed, which
sometimes brings out patriarchal habits and efforts
to re-establish traditional roles — even by force if
necessary. In a situation where men are unsure of
themselves, they often become skeptical about their**

PHOTO: UNHCR/L. GUBB

Southeast Asian children watching TV.

wives. Their own feelings of inferiority can lead to their doubting the love or trustworthiness of their wives. When men mistrust their wives, they may restrict them and try to control them in an effort to boost their egos.[4]

Intergenerational problems are not uncommon within refugee families. Children become adjusted to the new society more rapidly than their parents and must often act as a bridge between their parents and the new culture, assuming a role that is unknown in many traditional societies. Tensions between parent and child can then develop, with many refugee women feeling inadequate and unable to function in the new environment. Older refugee women may be particularly susceptible to feelings of isolation caused by these intergenerational tensions. A 70-year-old Vietnamese woman stated, 'How pitiful I am! I came here in 1975 with my daughter's family. I live with my daughter, son-in-law and grandchildren but I feel lonely. None of the kids likes to be near me because grandmom and grandchildren don't understand each other.'[5]

The change in family roles is often accompanied by the loss of traditional support systems for women:

Exile frequently entails the loss of traditional support systems upon which a woman refugee would normally rely. The absence of friends and extended family can be exceedingly painful. It may also disrupt the way the woman is accustomed to organizing her life. For example, a woman who has previously relied upon family members to care for her children while she is otherwise occupied may find that without this support her opportunities in the resettlement country considerably diminish.

The loss of neighbours and friends can

also limit a woman's possibilities. It is not uncommon for refugees to come from closely knit communities where neighbours provided both friendship and needed assistance. The loss of these intimate relationships is difficult for women refugees, particularly when they are resettled in a community with a more impersonal concept of neighborhood.[6]

The traumatic experiences of many refugee women further affect their ability to cope in a new culture. Some refugee women, as we have seen in Chapter 3, have been raped, tortured and sexually abused. They may have experienced the violent deaths of family members. Those refugee women who have had these experiences, may suffer from post-traumatic stress disorder. In common with refugees in camps, resettled refugees may suffer from depression, anxiety, intrusive thoughts, disassociation or psychic numbing, hyper-alertness, and sleeping and eating disorders. Surveys examining the mental health needs of refugees in the United States have found that single heads of household, widows and single women are particularly at risk.[7]

Language is a formidable barrier when refugee women first enter industrialized countries. Upon arrival, few speak the language of their adopted nations. A large household survey of South-East Asian refugees resettled in the United States showed, for example, that 64 per cent of new arrivals spoke no English at the time of entry into the US, with women having significantly less English language skills than men.[8]

Industrialized countries generally provide language training for refugees at no cost to the individual, though the actual mechanisms differ from one country to another. The United States, for example, requires that refugees from certain countries take up to six months of language

instruction and cultural orientation, prior to entry, at processing centres overseas, and also funds state governments to provide language training after resettlement; Australia tends to use reception centres where the English language is taught; while other countries offer classes through the regular school system or in community-based organizations.

Not surprisingly, language instruction has emerged as an effective means of acquiring a new language. A survey in the United States compared English language acquisition among those enrolled in full-time classes; those who combined classes and employment; those working and not enrolled in classes; and those participating neither in jobs nor classes. At the end of six months, the gains in English language displayed by those in full-time instruction were significantly greater than those in employment, who in turn had made better progress than those who were in neither.[9]

Access to language instruction has been shown to vary by gender, with women enrolling in classes at a lower rate than men. Younger refugees are also more likely to receive training, while those over the age of 50 are the least likely to be enrolled. Of all categories of refugees, therefore, older women are clearly the least likely to receive language instruction.[10]

The acquisition of the new language by home-bound women is particularly difficult, and proficiency in speaking will be a prime problem for them as they will have little opportunity to use it.

Barriers to women's access to language training include cultural constraints on women attending classes or participating in other activities outside the house. Women who want to enrol in and attend classes must also overcome practical problems, such as the need for day care and transport. The design of some language training programmes is also at fault: programmes may be geared towards an academic level of study unattainable for women with no previous education and who require basic survival skills as a first step in adjusting to the new culture. Or class hours may conflict with household or work demands.

These barriers also affect access to other forms of education. A study of education programmes for refugee women states:

Refugee women enter education programmes in the country of resettlement at a severe disadvantage. The vast majority have been excluded from educational experiences at home by a combination of factors: cultural, religious, social and legal customs and gender stereotyping.[11]

A study of refugee women in Britain described the education system as highly structured according to age groups and formal entry routes:

It lacks flexibility towards foreign qualifications and non-English speaking students.... Nowhere in Britain are there enough nursery places available to meet existing demand. Refugee families are expected to compete for the few facilities available. However, the cost of childcare is out of the reach of most refugee families, and the state provision is too selective and competitive to benefit them in any significant way.... Another problem is the frequent clash between college hours and children's school hours, making getting children to and from school impossible, thus excluding many women from study.[12]

Failure to learn the new language clearly reduces refugee women's ability to cope with the new society. A survey in Australia found that refugee women considered acquisition of the English language a pre-

Iraqi women learning German with teacher.

PHOTO: UNHCR/A. HOLLMAN

requisite for active involvement in other aspects of national life.[13] In most industrialized countries, to be reasonably conversant with the new language is necessary for obtaining employment, and also helps women better understand the rights and benefits to which they may be entitled.

Problems in language acquisition often lead to isolation; refugee women become housebound and must depend on their husbands and children for social intercourse. A study in Denmark described a typical case:

Presently Ms S. is isolated at home, occupied with the care of the baby, while her husband attends a vocational training course, being away for the most part of the day. She has no Sri Lankan or Danish friends.... Since she does not attend the Danish Refugee Council (DRC) language school, she is not only prevented from learning the Danish language, but is also cut off from contact with other refugees in and outside of the classroom, e.g., at social gatherings arranged by the Danish Refugee Council staff. She has no opportunities of obtaining relevant information which could help her out of her isolation, e.g., regarding special language classes for mothers with young children.[14]

Employment problems also affect refugee women's ability to adjust and integrate in their new country. In most industrialized countries, women's participation in the labour force has become very common. Most families require two household incomes, and refugee families are no exception. One study in the United States, for example, found that refugee families had great difficulty in becoming economically self-sufficient unless there were multiple wage-earners in the household.[15]

Experiences differ according to country, age and previous education as to the extent of employment among refugee women. Studies in the United States have found that relatively few refugee women seek outside employment but those who do are normally successful.[16] A study in Norway found similar patterns among women from Yugoslavia, but showed a lower employment rate among Chilean refugee women and high levels of what was referred to as 'hidden unemployment' among all groups.[17]

Barriers to seeking and obtaining employment are similar to those discussed regarding language training. First, cultural constraints can be formidable. For refugee women from many developing countries, outside employment may mean a radical change in lifestyle. The women may be working outside their home for the first time and this, in turn, may lead to changed relationships with their spouses. For their part, husbands may be frustrated by their inability to provide sufficiently for their families. Even refugee women from other industrialized countries who were themselves employed there may see paid work in their new country as culturally different. For those from centrally-planned, communist states, the competition and market-orientation of Western economies may be particularly difficult to understand and accommodate.

The need for child-care services is acute among many resettled women who wish to work, while lack of this service impedes access to other services as well. In some cases there are long waiting-lists for available day-care spaces; in others refugee families are reluctant to use the mainstream facilities. The Danish study referred to above described one woman's dilemma:

Mrs S. is hesitant about leaving the baby in a Danish nursery, having in fact turned down an offer of a nursery place when the baby was three months old. She worries that the culturally alien

environment, the Danish teachers, the different methods of child-care and feeding, and the Danish children, will not understand the baby's needs.[18]

When refugee women are employed, families use a wide variety of child-care mechanisms: some may use formal day-care programmes, others have relatives and friends care for their children. Many families arrange a staggered work schedule, with one parent caring for the children while the other works.

A further impediment to employment relates to women who have skills and prior education and/or work experience. They may have difficulty in applying their educational background and working experience in a new setting. The Danish study described these problems as:

- insufficient knowledge of qualifications required in Denmark, primarily of Danish language and cultural codes (general as well as in specific branches of professions and general labour market);

- cultural difference, e.g., between educational systems, ways of learning and attitudes towards work, differences between formal and informal learning systems. In Denmark the educational system and labour-market is characterized by a high degree of formalization, in contrast to the situation in most of the refugees' homelands;

- physical and technological differences between the Danish production system and labour market and those of the refugees, which make many of the refugees' job-categories meaningless in a Danish context.

Under-employment may be the result of difficulties in transforming prior education and skills into current labour market needs. As the Norwegian study previously referred to (p. 81) noted:

The average Chilean woman in our study is young, well-educated and urban in orientation. Although the occupational profile is similar to that of the Norwegian female population, the Chilean woman tends to end up in jobs considerably below her occupational and educational background. The Chilean woman who does work, does so full time in a low income job she dislikes.... As a result many have low family incomes and poor standards of living.[19]

Finding safe and affordable housing is a problem facing almost all refugees. Scandinavian countries and the Netherlands have good records of providing subsidized housing for refugees, but most countries provide either private housing or a combination of public and private accommodation for new arrivals. The provision of public housing can have its drawbacks; for example, where there are long waiting lists, citizens may express hostility towards refugees who are moved to the top of the queue. Also, public housing in some countries may be dilapidated and dangerous. One Cuban exile in the United States reported:

My parents live in low-income housing in the middle of a poor... neighbourhood. My parents do not go for walks. It is nothing short of outrageous to me that the government would place weak, old people in environments where they will meet with hostility. It shows an appalling degree of cultural insensitivity. To my parents, and to other old people in their situation, this is yet one more example of their helplessness and one further bizarre trait of this strange land.[20]

Refugees may be unable to afford to rent better accommodation, particularly that in safer neighbourhoods.

The new environment may be so frightening that even life in a refugee camp may seem good in comparison: 'I visit Chantha at 183rd Street in the Bronx, a tough neighbourhood by any standards and certainly different than anything she has ever known. At times we laugh about times in Khao-I-Dang as though they were the good old days'.[21]

Another problem militating against refugee women adjusting successfully to the new society is their health status. They often arrive with pre-existing conditions related to their refugee experience. Aside from the physical results of torture and abuse, they may have suffered from long bouts of malnutrition, physical exhaustion from the trek to a country of first asylum, repeated occurrences of malaria or other diseases, and the effects of parasites. In addition, many refugee women have had multiple pregnancies, so closely spaced that their health is jeopardized.

Once in an industrialized country, access to necessary health care may be a problem. In some countries, the issue is financial. Health care is not provided universally to the residents of the country, and refugee families may lack sufficient resources to pay for medical services. In the United States, for example, many entry-level jobs pay no health insurance costs. Only those who are unemployed and living much below the poverty standard are eligible for publicly funded health care; refugees, like many nationals, may be unwilling to take employment for fear of losing this public benefit.

Even where no financial barriers to health care exist, there are other impediments to effective use of available resources. Health facilities may have an inadequate translation and interpretation capacity. Refugees report reliance on their children to serve as translators. Yet, it may be very difficult for refugee women to discuss their medical problems, particularly gynaecological ones, through their children.

The services themselves may be seen as inappropriate from the refugee point of view. In many refugee cultures, for example, the Western concept of mental health therapy does not exist. Even where services are needed, the refugees may be reluctant to utilize them unless efforts are made to make them more understandable and culturally accessible.

Even the prospect of death can be an adjustment issue for refugees. In a study of older refugees in the United States, a 64-year-old Vietnamese woman who has had heart problems said that at times her thoughts turn to death. Although it holds no terror for her, the prospect of being buried in the cemetery next to Americans with no fellow Vietnamese nearby makes her uneasy. She says:

I am not afraid to die. But I would like to have enough money to be buried in the Vietnamese Senior Citizens cemetery. I would feel comfortable there. If I were buried elsewhere, I would not be able to talk with Americans next to me because I do not speak English.[22]

HELP IN ADJUSTMENT ☐ A theme that runs consistently through successful programmes for refugee women is empowerment. Refugee women in industrialized countries, no less than those still in camps, must participate in the design and implementation of programmes aimed at adaptation and integration into their new societies. By their very survival refugee women have shown their resilience. Even more important, they have much to offer to their new countries.

I never realized how strong I am. I always thought I was dependent on others. Now I know I can manage on my own. I feel strong deep inside. I want to encourage other refugee women to know that they can find confidence and hope.[23]

PHOTO: P. DELOCHE

Vietnamese woman with a newspaper.

A newsletter produced by Refugee Women in Development (RefWID, a refugee-women run organization), in seven different languages, explains the importance of empowerment to its refugee audience:

When we talk about equal opportunity for women we mean empowering them to employ their capabilities and talents, to contribute to their families' betterment and that of the world, and to make decisions about their own lives. While all human beings are fundamentally born equal, socio-economic conditions, gender, and other factors divide them into groups of privileged and underprivileged citizens. Gender discrimination is indefensible both on moral and practical grounds as witnessed by the participation of women in many societies throughout history.[24]

Empowerment of refugee women has been promoted in a number of ways in industrialized countries.

One mechanism builds relationships between refugee women and other women in the community. *Le Comité Intermouvements auprès des Evacués* (CIMADE) and the *Groupe d'Accueil et Solidarité* (GAS) sponsored a meeting at which refugee women from various countries were invited to share their experiences in their home country and in France. The goal was to identify the specific problems of refugee women. A participant noted:

Further dialogues followed which were fruitful, as French women and refugee women listened to each other's experiences and forged links. During this time, we reflected on the future of our group and decided to become an autonomous association. For us, the designation 'association' means we are in solidarity with each other. We express our feelings; we question ourselves about

**our own problems; and we understand
and feel ourselves to be united by what
we have in common.**[25]

A similar meeting was held in the United
States in 1990 at which refugee and US-
born women compared their experiences.
The refugees were surprised to learn that
some of their frustrations with life in the
United States, particularly dealing with
discrimination, the problems of juggling
both work and household responsibilities,
and the reluctance of male members of
their families to share in home responsibilities, were shared by American women.
The American women gained a better
understanding of the special barriers faced
by the refugee women.[26]

A second strategy uses women refugee
self-help groups. The Women's Association
of Hmong and Lao, Inc. (WAHL), in
Minnesota, is run by and for refugee
women. It was founded in 1981 to serve
these women and their families and to
strengthen the relationship among Hmong,
Lao and American women. Through literacy classes, ethnic meals, support groups,
socialization activities and information/
referral services, WAHL helps reduce the
isolation of refugee women. It also assists
them to gain access to community
resources and services.

A refugee women's network in Chicago
involves refugee women from a number of
different countries. It was conceived to
increase confidence and self-sufficiency
among refugee women, to help them
effectively identify problems and address
needs by building support networks, to
strengthen leadership among refugee
women, and to nurture co-operation
among the different ethnic groups.
Women's specialists have been hired at
five service centres to organize activities
for refugee women. Group activities have
included workshops on birth control,
dressing for cold weather, women's health

concerns, home safety, nutrition, and the
public school system. Home visits are an
essential part of the programme.

A pamphlet published by the Foreign
Women's Group in Norway illustrates a
third method of empowerment. The focus
of the pamphlet is on the rights of immigrant women. It covers education,
employment, health, housing, marriage
and divorce, social welfare, violence
against women, and child care. It also provides addresses of institutions that can be
contacted for more information or assistance.

RefWID has established training programmes for refugee women, and for
those providing services, about refugee
women's needs and ways to address them;
a particular concern has been domestic
violence. A curriculum has been produced
to give more information to social service
providers and others working with
refugees. In collaboration with the
Indochinese Psychiatric Clinic associated
with Harvard University, RefWID is
assessing the effect of rape on refugee
women and their families. The Quilting
Bee, published in Washington, DC, in
numerous languages reflecting the origins
of refugee women in the United States,
provides information about the rights of
women. Special programmes have been
established in a number of places to
address the barriers that women face in
obtaining language training and employment. A 'mentoring' project for refugee
women has sought to bring refugee and
American women together to help orient
refugee women to life in the United
States. Called 'First Steps for Women',
the programme is aimed at illiterate
women who know no English. A refugee
woman is paired with a mentor who helps
her learn independent living skills, particularly through the acquisition of English
language skills. Communication is facili-
tated by use of pictures, simple books and

by pointing to household items to learn vocabulary.

STEPS TO BE TAKEN TO ENHANCE THE ADJUSTMENT OF REFUGEE WOMEN IN INDUSTRIALIZED COUNTRIES

- Implement Women-at-risk programmes to facilitate the admission of women who urgently require resettlement.

- Improve and reduce the length of procedures for determining refugee status in asylum procedures. (See recommendations in Chapter 3 for greater detail.)

- Facilitate the empowerment of refugee women through support for self-help groups, provision of information about the rights of refugee women, and increased collaboration between refugee women and women already resident in the country.

- Improve the capacity of social, education and employment services to address the needs of refugee women, including the provision of child-care services, training programmes, special provisions for homebound women, etc.

- Provide interpretation and translation services for refugee women to enhance their ability to access health and other services.

- Recognize the diverse range of skills and prior experience which refugee women bring to their new countries. Assist women to adapt professionally while providing opportunities for women who have had no previous outside work experience.

Language training for homebound women takes a number of forms. Tutors sometimes come directly to their homes; other programmes utilize community centres which also provide child care. These centres are often located within walking distance of the refugees' homes and therefore facilitate their attendance. One programme has provided workshops at a local centre that address health, education and cultural topics, including an introduction to the new country's educational system to enable mothers to understand their children's experiences. Courses in crime prevention are also given.[27]

Other programmes have focused on employment skills training. The US government, for example, funded a number of projects under the heading 'Multiple Wage Earner' programmes designed to help more than one member of a family obtain employment. Most of the projects offered child-care and transport in addition to the training. Generally, training was built on existing skills to the degree possible; for example, some programmes taught refugee women to operate power sewing machines.

Craft co-operatives have been another way to help refugee women augment their family income. Cottage Crafts, a language training and cottage industry/employment programme, served mainly Hmong women. The women received initial counselling in their own homes and volunteer tutors taught English. Because of the project, the Hmong established a co-operative oriental food and gift store. It also generated increased income for participants who obtained full- or part-time jobs.

CONCLUSION ☐ Admission to an industrialized country presents many challenges for refugee women. Whether they enter as asylum seekers or through a resettlement programme, whether they come from a developing or an industrialized country, issues of adjustment and integration must be resolved. Effective programmes have been established in a number of settings, programmes that can be used as models to improve efforts to help refugee women adapt to their new surroundings.

1 John Tenhula, 1991, pp. 122–3.
2 Noreen Spencer-Simmons, 1990, p. 20.
3 UNHCR, 1990a, p. 16.
4 Irmtraud Weissinger, in Ninette Kelly, 1989, p. 157.
5 Refugee Policy Group, 1988, Summary of a symposium on older refugees in the United States.
6 Ninette Kelly, 1989, p. 59.
7 Lewin/ICF and Refugee Policy Group, 1990.
8 Nathan Caplan, *et al*, 1985.
9 Northwest Regional Educational Laboratory, 1982–4.
10 Ibid.
11 World University Service in Ninette Kelly, 1989.
12 Ibid.
13 Eileen Pittaway, 1990.
14 Inger Boesen and Ken Pedersen, 1988, p. 5.
15 Nathan Caplan *et al*, 1985.
16 Susan Forbes, 1985, p. 6.
17 Suzanne Stiver Lie, 1983, p. 65.
18 Inger Boesen and Ken Pedersen, 1988.
19 Suzanne Stiver Lie, 1983.
20 Elzbieta Gozdziak, 1988, p. 26.
21 Abby Spero, 1985, p. 137.
22 Elzbieta Gozdziak, 1988, p. 38.
23 Helena Moussa, in Ninette Kelly, 1989, p. 152.
24 Refugee Women in Development, 1988.
25 Working Group on Refugee Women, Paris, in Ninette Kelly, 1989, p. 154.
26 Sponsored by the American Refugee Committee in Minnesota in October 1990.
27 Abby Spero, 1985, p. 139.

8 RESPONSES... AND SOLUTIONS?

The United Nations General Assembly, noting with great concern that women and children constitute the majority of refugees and displaced persons in most areas,...urges the international community to provide urgent and adequate assistance to all refugee and displaced women and to developing countries providing asylum or rehabilitation, especially the least developed and most seriously affected countries.[1]

FOLLOWING YEARS OF INATTENTION to the needs and resources of refugee and displaced women, a new awareness and willingness to take gender into account in policy development and implementation has emerged. This chapter reviews efforts to improve responses to refugee women in the UN system as well as by NGOs.

UN INITIATIVES ☐ In December 1975, the General Assembly proclaimed 1976–85 as the UN Decade for Women: Equality, Development and Peace. A World Plan of Action was adopted. By the end of five years, when a mid-decade review would be held, some minimum goals were to be met in terms of increased literacy, equal access to education, increased employment, equal eligibility for the vote, greater participation of women in policy-making, increased provision of health services, and recognition of the economic value of women's work at home. The World Plan of Action drew special attention to the situation of migrant women, recognizing that they faced special problems.

The mid-decade meeting took place in Copenhagen in July 1980. Specific resolutions relating to refugee and displaced women were adopted by that meeting. In addition to some general recommendations about the causes of refugee movements and the responsibilities of states to protect and assist refugees, regarding refugee women the report of the meeting:

- Strongly urged governments to bring to justice those who abuse refugee women and children and to take steps to prevent such abuses;

- Urged UNHCR, in co-operation with other concerned UN agencies, to establish programmes necessary for dealing with the special needs of displaced and refugee women, especially in the areas of health, education and employment;

- Urged UNHCR to develop and implement programmes of resettlement and family reunification, including special programmes for reuniting unaccompanied children with their families;

- Recommended that UNHCR increase the number of women at all levels of its staff and establish a high-level position of co-ordinator of women's programmes;

- Requested that family planning information and methods should be available on a voluntary and nationally acceptable basis to both refugee women and men.

More specifically, the Programme of Action for the second half of the decade called for assistance and counselling to women refugees, with an emphasis on the development of self-reliance; special health care measures and health counselling by women medical workers where necessary; supplemental feeding programmes for pregnant and lactating women; training and educational programmes including orientation, language and job training; income-generation programmes; and sufficient international personnel in refugee camps to discourage exploitation and attacks on refugee women.

Little progress was made in implementing these recommendations during the next five years. There were some efforts, however, to gain greater understanding of the needs of refugee women. For example, in 1981 the Intergovernmental Committee for Migration held a seminar on the adaptation and integration of refugee and migrant women.

The meeting in Nairobi marking the end of the decade on women served as an impetus for further action in 1985. In April of that year, UNHCR organized a Round Table on Refugee Women, which included a number of prominent women – cabinet ministers, ambassadors and others – who would be involved in the Nairobi meeting. Also, a number of governmental delegations made the issue a priority for discussion at Nairobi. The US government, for example, provided funds for a study of refugee women that was to develop recommendations its delegation could take to the Nairobi conference. NGOs came with specific recommendations for improvements as well.

In the years after the Nairobi end-of-decade meeting and the inclusion of specific reference to refugee women in the Forward Looking Strategies (paragraphs 298 and 299), interest in the issue of refugee women increased among donor governments and within UNHCR. In October 1985, for the first time, the Executive Committee of the UNHCR included this issue on its agenda and adopted a resolution (No. 36) on the protection of refugee women. In 1987, it called upon the High Commissioner to report in detail at its next session on the particular protection and assistance problems and needs of refugee women and on the concrete measures taken to meet them. In February 1988, UNHCR established a Steering Committee on Refugee Women, under the Chairmanship of the Deputy High Commissioner, to define, oversee and co-ordinate a process of assessing, strengthening and reorienting existing policies and programmes. Then, in August 1988, internal guidelines on the international protection of refugee women were issued to all substantive officers in the field and at headquarters.

A Note on Refugee Women was prepared for the meeting of the Executive Committee in 1988. The Note summarized the various protection and assistance issues facing refugee women and described the current and planned action of UNHCR. Field officers were requested to provide more detailed information and follow-up. The data systems for collecting information on refugees were reviewed with an aim to increase their capacity to record gender-specific information. Efforts were also begun to identify institutional changes needed to ensure that the needs of refugee women were systematically considered and addressed; to raise the level of visibility given to refugee women's issues; and to develop training materials to sensitize UNHCR, host country governments and NGO staff.

A new position was created to ensure that these activities were productive: a Senior Coordinator for Refugee Women. Canada provided a major impetus for this appointment and seconded a senior staff member to fill the position. Her duties include: co-ordinating and monitoring the process of integrating women's issues throughout the organization; preparing a policy framework to include refugee women in all levels of programme and project planning and implementation; reviewing existing programmes and procedures to ensure full participation of refugee women; identifying appropriate action-oriented research on specific women's issues; contributing to the review and assessment of protection and assistance programmes; and assisting in the development of training programmes on gender impact analysis. She reports directly to the High Commissioner's office.

The Report submitted to the Executive Committee in 1989 described continued problems for refugee women (particularly regarding physical protection) but it detailed progress at UNHCR in addressing the concerns:

- an evaluation of the protection guidelines found them to be of value and showed revisions needed to improve them;

- instructions had gone out to field offices that they must ensure that proposed programme plans addressed the special needs of refugee women and children and took into account the ways in which they could contribute to the success of refugee programmes;

- means of verifying the level of integration of women's concerns into programming were developed;

- an analytical framework for assessing the situation of refugee women was developed;

- the terms of reference for all field missions conducted by the Technical Support Unit included needs assessment of the situation of refugee women;

- the need for a primary health care approach with emphasis on women and children was reaffirmed and recommendations were made that at least 50 percent of the health workers be women;

- the special emergency needs of refugee women received increased attention in the UNHCR Handbook for Emergencies; and

- the needs of refugee women were to be taken into account in all refugee aid and development programmes and projects.

Recognizing the need for more information on refugee women, the Office embarked on several research projects on specific countries, and issues such as education. The Technical Support Service also engaged in several field missions aimed at assessing the situation of refugee women in specific locations, such as Guinea, Côte d'Ivoire and Hong Kong.

Recognizing the importance of trained and sensitive staff, UNHCR introduced a course in gender impact analysis for refugee assistance projects. The course is designed to ensure that project planners and other staff perform a thorough analysis of the situation of women in any refugee population, based on an examination of the gender-based division of socio-economic roles.

The Executive Committee reaffirmed the importance of continued progress in addressing the needs of refugee women. Its conclusions also noted the intention to include the protection of refugee women as a separate agenda item of the Sub-Committee of the Whole [Executive Committee] on International Protection. And, the Executive Committee requested UNHCR to provide a policy framework and organizational work plan to be submitted at its next session.

The major thrust of the policy statement later approved by the Executive Committee is the integration of considerations regarding the special needs and resources of refugee women into all aspects of UNHCR's protection and assistance activities. Referred to as mainstreaming, the policy seeks to ensure recognition that becoming a refugee affects women and men differently and that effective programming must recognize these differences. The policy further recognizes that refugee women must themselves participate in the planning and implementation of projects. Within this framework, women are to be thought of not just as vulnerable people requiring assistance but also as resources for their own and their communities' development. The full policy statement is included in Annex Two.

DISPLACED WOMEN AND THE UN SYSTEM □ Progress regarding internally displaced women has been markedly slower than even these steps. Issues still need to be resolved generally regarding the mandates of international organizations for providing assistance and protection to the internally displaced. Two recent international conferences, one on Southern Africa (SARRED) and the other on Central America (CIREFCA), highlighted the needs of this population.

A working group was formed to determine which UN agency would play the leading role in providing assistance to those internally displaced. The UN Development Programme (UNDP) Resident Representative has responsibility for co-ordinating efforts in the field. The Governing Council of the UNDP passed a resolution at its 1990 meeting authorizing UNDP to undertake the work. It allowed for the expenditure of US$500,000 in special programmes. The Governing Council also recommended a system-wide review of the UN's co-ordination of assistance to refugees, returnees and displaced persons. Subsequently, the Economic and Social Council (ECOSOC) passed a resolution requesting the Secretary-General to undertake the system-wide review.[2]

In its annual meeting, the UN Commission on Human Rights requested the Secretary-General both to include an examination of the protection issues involving displaced persons in the study and to:

submit an analytical report on internally displaced persons, taking into account the protection of human rights of internally displaced persons, based on information submitted by Governments, the specialized agencies, relevant United Nations organs, regional and intergovernmental organizations, the International Committee of the Red Cross and non-governmental organizations.[3]

In the interim, no UN agency has clear responsibility for providing assistance or protection to the internally displaced; the protection situation is particularly acute. UNDP removed its staff from Liberia and Somalia, for example, because it was too dangerous to operate its programmes there, leaving the displaced population, for which it was co-ordinating assistance, with no UN presence.

Given the tentative beginnings of any discussion about the needs of internally displaced persons and the role of the UN in relationship to them, it is not surprising that little attention has been given to the situation of specific sections of this population, such as women or children. The deliberations of the UN Commission on the Status of Women do provide a potential framework, however, for filling this gap, as described below.

THE UN COMMISSION ON THE STATUS OF WOMEN □ The thirty-fifth session of the Commission on the Status of Women provided a forum for heightening awareness of the situation of refugee and displaced women, particularly in the broader range of UN agencies. To prepare for the meeting, the Division for the Advancement of Women held an experts' meeting that outlined specific recommendations to improve the UN system's responsiveness to the needs of refugee women. The meeting involved UNHCR, UNRWA, UNICEF, various NGOs and other relevant organizations.

The Expert Group emphasized the importance of ensuring that the civil, political, social and cultural rights of refugee and displaced women and children are reaffirmed and backed by laws, policies and programmes. Governments, relevant UN agencies, and concerned NGOs were called upon to redouble their efforts to respond to the specific needs of refugee and displaced women and children, including urgently addressing the root causes of these situations.

The Expert Group provided detailed recommendations to improve both emergency and longer-term assistance. Greater attention needs to be given to combating malnutrition, improving health, increasing access to safe drinking water, constructing adequate and appropriate shelter, and providing the mechanisms for increased self-reliance through education programmes, employment and income-generation. Recognizing the close link between protection and assistance measures, the group recommended that protection concerns be borne in mind when planning and implementing assistance programmes.

The Commission, in its March 1991 meeting, adopted many of the Expert Groups' recommendations. The resolutions requested the UN and other inter-governmental organizations, governments, NGOs and funding agencies that play a role in the protection of and/or assistance to refugees and displaced persons, to adopt a policy statement on refugee and displaced women and children, including a time frame for implementation. These women and children should be fully integrated into every aspect of that agency's mandate and programmes. The Commission also requested the Secretary-General to ensure that the system-wide review of assistance assess, in particular, the ability of UN organizations to address the situation of women and children.

The international community was urged by the Commission to give priority to extending international protection to refugee and displaced women and children. It also urged implementation of measures to ensure greater protection from physical violence, sexual abuse, abduction and those circumstances which force women and children into illegal or dangerous activities.

Further, the Commission urged the full participation of refugee and displaced women in the process of assessing their needs, planning and implementing programmes, and the recruitment of staff, particularly women, in order to provide appropriate assistance and protection. Key staff of relevant organizations should receive training to help them respond more effectively to the presence and needs of refugee and displaced women. The resolutions are included in Annex Two (pp. 99–120).

NON-GOVERNMENTAL ORGANIZATIONS

☐ NGOs have been pivotal forces in lobbying governments and the UN system to take needed actions to improve responses to refugee women's situations. The NGOs have also looked at their own roles in implementing policies that will allow for more effective programmes for these women. Prior to the Nairobi conference, NGOs in a number of countries wrote, and held meetings about the situation of refugee women, and promoted greater attention to their situation. Concerned organizations participated in the NGO meetings surrounding the Nairobi conference. Workshops focused specifically on this issue.

Internationally, the focus of NGO involvement has been the NGO Working Group on Refugee Women. The Working Group, a coalition of interested individuals from about 100 NGOs throughout the world, keeps its members informed of developments and convenes meetings to coincide with the executive committee meetings at UNHCR.

An international consultation organized by the Working Group was held in

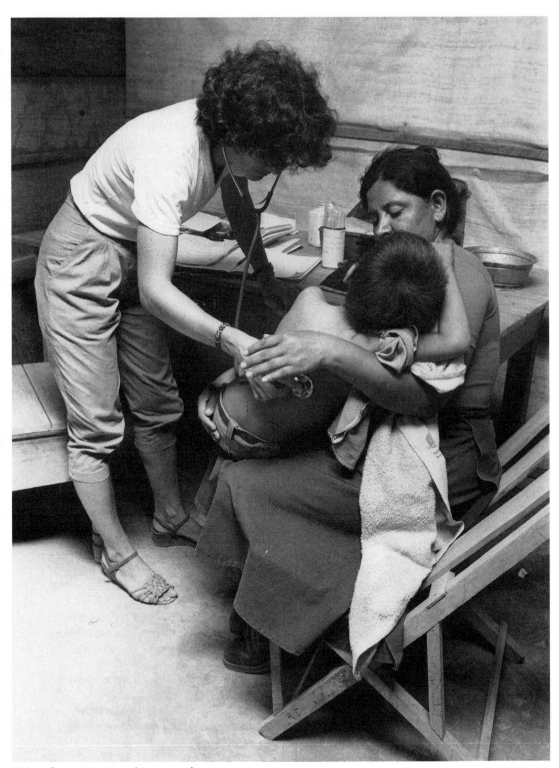

NGO worker assisting Central American refugees.

November 1988. This brought together about 150 representatives from refugee women's groups, NGOs, intergovernmental organizations, and governments to consider how refugee women's issues can be more effectively addressed by the international community. The meeting was organized around five major themes: protection, health, education, employment and cultural adjustment; participants developed specific recommendations pertaining to these areas. Following the consultation, a report was prepared, entitled 'Working with Refugee Women: A Practical Guide', which includes analyses of the five themes, specific recommendations for action, background papers, and personal stories by and about refugee women. The NGO Working Group, under the secretariat of the Norwegian Refugee Council, has remained a major impetus for improvements in the situation of and responses of these women.

Groups have also developed in individual countries, some examining the policies within their own countries and others focusing on international assistance and protection. For example, the Women's Commission for Refugee Women and Children was established in the United States to speak in support of improved policies and programmes for refugee and displaced women. An Australian National Consultative Committee on Refugee Women was formed with the aim of improving the quality of life of refugee women, networking both internationally and nationally and being the focal point for the expression of the concerns of refugee women. A similar coalition has been established in Canada.

FROM POLICY TO IMPLEMENTATION
☐ The development of policies and guidelines related to the protection of and assistance to refugee women and children provides a useful framework for increasing

the capacity of the international system to respond to the needs of these populations. The test of the success of these policies and guidelines will be in their implementation. Here, much remains to be done:

● mechanisms must be developed to actually integrate refugee women's and children's issues into all stages of programme planning, implementation, monitoring and evaluation;

● country-specific and sector-specific policies and procedures must be reviewed and revised, as necessary, to reflect the policies on refugee women and children;

● needs assessments and data collection must provide a more accurate representation of the refugee population; and

● more effective and creative programmes must be implemented if the needs of refugee women and children are to be met.

Improvements in staffing and training are key to achieving the other changes needed to respond more effectively to the needs of refugee women. In particular, female staff (UN, NGO, host country and refugee) must be recruited, particularly where it is culturally appropriate for only women to work with refugee women. In 1990 the Permanent Working Group on the Situation of Women in UNHCR reported inadequacies in staffing:

The status of women in UNHCR remains extremely feeble. Though [the proportion of women is] high among the G[eneral] S[upport] staff, the proportions are considerably lower than those of males in the [professional] categories. The presence of women in the most senior grades, in particular, leaves much to be desired.[4]

The Working Group recommended

Ethiopian refugee girl.

increasing the proportion of women professional staff at both the central and field levels in the interest of equity as well as effective performance. Noting that the majority of refugees are women and children, the Working Group underlined the important role that women staff at UNHCR could play in ensuring greater participation of refugee women.

A further priority for UNHCR is the training of its own staff and that of its implementing partners to help them respond more effectively. 'A Framework for People-oriented Planning in Refugee Situations' has been developed to facilitate this training, which is designed to provide staff with 'a framework for analysing the socio-cultural factors in a refugee society which can influence the success of planned activities'.[5] The training programme helps staff to analyse social and economic roles, understand how these will affect and be affected by the refugee situation, analyse the resources refugees controlled and used before and since becoming refugees, and plan programmes designed to maximize the participation at all phases of both women and men.

It should be kept in mind that adoption of the policy on refugee women by UNHCR and its effective implementation will solve only part of the problem. Similar policies must be designed by a range of other institutions. A large number of refugee and displaced women and children do not fall within the UNHCR mandate, including internally displaced persons, women and children in camps along the Thai–Cambodian border, Palestinian women and children, among others. They are assisted, when assisted, by other UN agencies, including the UN Development Programme, the UN Border Relief Operation and the UN Relief and Works Agency for Palestine Refugees in the Near East. Each agency has had valuable experience in providing assistance (though less so protection) to refugee women and needs to share these experiences with the others. It is through such co-ordinated development of programmes that improved responses to the needs of refugee women will come.

Even within UNHCR-administered camps, other institutions play prominent roles. Host country ministries (either those created specially for handling refugee matters, or existing ones such as the health or education ministry) co-ordinate and sometimes directly provide services to refugees. Their immigration departments are generally responsible for interviewing applicants for refugee status. Non-governmental agencies serve as the operational partner of UNHCR in many locations. They are responsible for health services, supplemental feeding programmes, education, skills-training, income-generation projects, and so on. The World Food Programme (WFP) is responsible for distribution of the basic food ration in many refugee situations. Other UN bodies (UNICEF, WHO, UNESCO) also have roles. Donor governments provide financial support for these various programmes as well as providing leadership in policy formulation; and the list could continue.

The sensitivity of these institutions to issues relating to refugee and displaced women and children must be increased. Their capacity to integrate these issues into their own planning and programme implementation must also be developed. With regard to internally displaced persons, in particular, broader issues of protection and assistance must be worked through if women and children are not to suffer unnecessarily.

CONCLUSION ☐ The special needs and resources of refugee women are now well-documented. The challenge for the future is to translate our improved understanding of their situation into concrete, effective programmes which will help them live in safety and dignity. If any lesson is to be learned from the past, it is the importance of including refugee women in all aspects of programme design and implementation. They are the best judges of their needs and aspirations.

1   UN General Assembly, 1980.
2   UN Economic and Social Council, 1990.
3   UN Commission on Human Rights, 1991.
4   UNHCR, 1990g, p.2.
5   UNHCR, 1991.

ANNEX I
SUGGESTIONS FOR USE

THIS BOOK PROVIDES a basis for study and further activities. Annex 1 contains some guidelines on organizing meetings and discussion groups to promote greater awareness and understanding of the situation of refugee and displaced women. Gatherings may be brief informal meetings or longer and more detailed seminars and workshops. They can focus on a specific refugee situation (e.g. refugee women in Africa) or a set of issues facing refugees worldwide (e.g. refugee protection).

The participants can include experts as well as people with interest in but little prior experience of the issues. Efforts should be made to seek out people in such diverse fields as health care, education, and law, to name but three, who have the necessary skills to improve the protection and assistance of refugee and displaced women. Refugee women should be included in the discussion wherever possible. Beyond drawing in needed skills, meetings on refugee and displaced women can help focus the compassion many of us feel for uprooted women.

PLAN FOR A TWO-HOUR MEETING

Refugee situations are often in the news. People seeing short television clips of dying women and children often want to know how they can help. A meeting that provides up-to-date information about a newsworthy refugee situation can often be a vehicle for educating people about the longer-term issues. It can be aimed at a general audience or groups whose pro-fessional interests interesect with those needed to respond effectively to the situation of refugee women.

Another approach in a short meeting is to remind participants that refugees live in their own communities, and can be found in almost every country. Refugee women who have been resettled often have interesting stories to tell about their own experiences. Similarly, women who have worked or volunteered for service in refugee camps can be found in many locations. A panel composed of refugee women and workers may be a way to educate others in a relatively short time by drawing out the common themes in personal experiences.

ONE-DAY MEETING

A one-day meeting provides greater opportunity to discuss and assess issues. Examples of suitable subjects for a one-day meeting are: Refugee Women and Protection; From Relief to Development, Serving the Needs of Refugee Women; and the Adaptation and Integration of Refugee Women in Our Community. Typically, a one-day session begins with an introduction to the issue, continues with speakers, and concludes with discussion.

Using this basic plan, a one-day meeting on 'Refugee Women and Protection' could have the following agenda:
- Welcome and Introduction.
- Speakers on the protection situation of refugee women, drawing on specific cases. Speakers could include a UNHCR public information officer, women who have worked with refugee women and refugee women themselves.
- Panel discussion of the role of relief and development organizations in promoting greater protection for refugee women. Speakers could include representatives

of agencies working in the health area, education, income-generation and other assistance sectors. The panel could also include a representative of a human rights organization concerned with women's rights, who could speak about co-operative activities between refugee organizations and human rights organizations.

- Discussion, with recommendations for follow-up.

Extracts from Chapter 3 of this book could form the basis of fact sheets to be given to participants. Displays of photographs and maps would help focus the discussion.

A THREE-DAY SEMINAR/WORKSHOP

A longer session allows not only for discussion of a wider set of issues but the development of recommendations and plans of action. Such extended meetings can include plenary sessions attended by all participants and smaller workshops which focus on a specific issue. This format allows for presentations by experts and discussion by participants.

Presented here is a suggested schedule for a three-day meeting for development agencies staff:

PLAN FOR A SEMINAR

First day	Second day	Third day
09.00 Registration	**09.00** The Protection Situation of Refugee Women: The Role of Relief and Development Workers	**09.00** Working Groups to Develop Plans of Action
09.30 Welcome/Introductions		These can look at sectoral plans of action, institutional roles and relationships, policy and so on
10.00 Refugee Women as a Development Issue	Presentation followed by discussion	
The meeting begins with a presentation that makes the case for treating refugee issues as a women in development concern. The presentation is followed by questions and answers.	**10.30** Sectoral Workshops (as per first day)	**12.00** Lunch
	13.00 Lunch	**14.00** Reports of Working Groups
	14.30 The Search for Durable Solutions	**16.00** Conclusions and Recommendations
11.30 Panel on the Situation of Refugee Women in Specific Developing Countries	Panel composed of government and UN officials, NGOs' representatives and refugee women	**17.00** Adjourn meeting
13.00 Lunch		
14.30 Sectoral Workshops: Health; Education; Income generation	**16.00** Break	
	16.30 Reports from Sectoral Workshops	
These workshops are overlapping; they will be repeated so that each participant can take part in at least two.	**18.00** Adjourn for the day	
17.00 Film		
18.00 Adjourn for the day		

ANNEX II

RELEVANT

UN DOCUMENTATION

UNHCR POLICY ON REFUGEE WOMEN
submitted by the High Commissioner

I INTRODUCTION

1 The Executive Committee has adopted four general conclusions relating specifically to refugee women:

- During its thirty-sixth session in 1985, the Executive Committee adopted conclusion No. 39, entitled 'Refugee Women and International Protection', in which it stressed the need for UNHCR and host governments to give particular attention to the international protection of refugee women.

- At its thirty-eighth session in 1987, the Executive Committee in its 'General Conclusions on International Protection' noted that refugee women had protection and assistance needs which necessitated special attention in order to improve existing protection and assistance programmes, and called on all States and concerned agencies to support the efforts of the Office in this regard. It also recognized the need for reliable information and statistics about refugee women in order to increase awareness about their situation.

- In 1988, at its thirty-ninth session, the Executive Committee adopted a conclusion entitled 'Refugee Women' which elaborates further on the special vulnerability of refugee women and the particular problems that they face, notably in the area of physical security, and noted the need to promote the participation of refugee women as agents as well as beneficiaries of programmes on their behalf. The conclusion also stressed the need for 'an active senior-level steering committee' on refugee women to co-ordinate, integrate and oversee the assessment, reorientation and strengthening of existing policies and programmes in favour of refugee women, whilst ensuring that such efforts were culturally appropriate and resulted in the full integration of the women concerned. There was also emphasis on the necessity for public information on the issue of refugee women and the need for the development of training modules on the subject, in order to increase awareness of the specific needs of refugee women and the practical means of addressing these needs.

- At its fortieth session in 1989, the Executive Committee adopted a conclusion on refugee women reiterating concern about physical safety and sexual exploitation. It also called for a policy framework for the next stages in mainstreaming women's issues within the organization with particular attention to the need for female field workers to facilitate the participation of refugee women. It reaffirmed the conclusions of the thirty-ninth session regarding refugee women, called for expanded training and the development of a methodology to systematically address gender issues in refugee programmes.

- In addition to the Executive Committee conclusion, UNHCR, as a United Nations agency, is obliged to implement the Nairobi Forward Looking Strategies for the Advancement of Women. Both the above noted conclusions and the strategies reflect the international community's recognition that programmes which are planned or implemented without the consultation or participation of half the target population (the women) cannot be effective and could, inadvertently, have a negative impact on their socio-economic situation. This paper draws together the various Executive Committee conclusions and applicable United Nations resolutions into a policy framework for future action aimed at improving the situation of refugee women.

2 UNHCR's unique functions of providing protection to refugees and helping find durable solutions to their problems imply specific obligations with regard to programmes for refugee women who represent, with their dependants, over 80 per cent of the beneficiaries of UNHCR's assistance programmes. The present paper sets out the policy framework for the elaboration of an organizational work plan for the integration of refugee women into programming* and project activities. The Office's international protection activities on behalf of refugee women are considered in more detail in a separate paper, document EC/SCP/59, which also discusses some of the considerations in the area of protection and assistance on which the formulations of the present paper are based. The Executive Committee's conclusions on this paper will be incorporated into the organizational work plan.

3 The present paper introduces, in Part III, the underlying principles of the policy. These are the integration of the resources and needs of refugee women into all aspects of programming, rather than creating special women's projects, and the need for each staff member to

ensure that this takes place in his or her area of competence. In Part IV, the paper outlines the organizational goals for refugee women, that is, the activities which UNHCR is required to carry out in this connection under its mandate. In Part V are outlined the policy objectives, that is, the interpretation of the organizational goals at the policy level. Finally, Part VI sets out the operational objectives of the policy, that is, a series of activities at the project level to ensure the practical implementation of the policy. These objectives are based on the Nairobi Forward Looking Strategies for the Advancement of Women and the conclusions adopted by the Executive Committee since its thirty-ninth session.

II GENERAL

4 The policy set out in this document is premised on the recognition that becoming a refugee affects men and women differently and that effective programming must recognize these differences. Furthermore, to understand fully the protection needs and assistance resources of the refugee population, and to encourage dignity and self-sufficiency, refugee women themselves must participate in planning and implementing projects. Socio-cultural and economic roles can, to a great extent, determine the pattern of such participation. Traditional roles are often disrupted and then either undermined or reinforced by the refugee situation. It is, therefore, essential that organizations working with refugees recognize that special initiatives must often be taken to ensure that

---

* 'Programmes' refer to all aspects of UNHCR's activities including protection, assistance and durable solutions.

all refugees have the opportunity to contribute to the activities planned for them.

III THE BASIC PRINCIPLE: MAINSTREAMING/INTEGRATION

5 It is the intention of UNHCR to integrate the resources and needs of refugee women in all aspects of programme planning and implementation. This does not mean that separate 'women's' projects are to be initiated or added on to existing general programme activities. Nor does it mean that responsibility for this process will rest with one work unit. It is the responsibility of each staff member to ensure that it takes place within his or her area of competence. The following terms and definitions are useful in understanding this concept.

What are programmes or projects which mainstream/integrate refugee women?

6 Any intervention, emergency, mid- or long-term, will have a different impact on men, women and children. Protection and assistance programmes or projects which mainstream/integrate refugee women are based on an explicit recognition of this fact. In activities which mainstream refugee women, action is taken to enable refugee women to participate and make a positive contribution.

7 Planning for such projects includes more than women's social role as daughter/wife/mother. It highlights a woman's economic role as income-earner for herself and her family, producer and/or manager of food, provider of fuel and water, and her religious, cultural and political activities. These roles, and, even more importantly, the change in these roles created by the

refugee situation are frequently overlooked by planners. Consequently, interventions which do not take these factors into consideration may be inappropriate to women, tend to isolate them from mainstream project activities, further reinforce their dependency, and force them into unaccustomed social or economic roles.

8 The concept of mainstreaming refugee women arose from a better understanding of the implications of the division of labour between women and men. A programme which integrates refugee women will have taken into consideration factors influenced by the male/female roles in a society and included these in the planned activity with a view to benefiting the whole target population, not marginalizing a portion of it. Refugee women are emphasized because, inadvertently, planners have often overlooked them. Until needs assessment and participation of all segments of a target group are integral to good planning, attention must be consistently drawn to refugee women. This will ensure that they are included in mainstream activities, not made peripheral to them or segregated into 'women's projects'.

Projects that focus on refugee women as a target group are not necessarily mainstreaming/integrating projects

9 The provision of goods to refugee women, that is, when women are passive recipients of shelter or food aid, is not in itself integrating refugee women. Neither is the provision of services to refugee women and their families necessarily an integrating activity. However, the provision of goods and services to refugee women may be part of a project or programme which main-

streams or integrates refugee women. For example, if women as well as men are consulted on the type of shelter required and the resources available to set up and maintain this shelter, then they have been integrated in the overall project. If women are asked about traditional diet, food preparation, and participate in the distribution and allocation of food, then they have been integrated into this activity.

10 By interpreting UNHCR's policy and operational objectives, the meaning of mainstreaming in a project becomes clearer. For example, projects may:

- identify constraints to women's participation related to project delivery procedures;

- respond to the initiatives of refugee women to improve their own situation;

- make available appropriate technologies that alleviate time and energy demands on refugee women;

- collect statistics indicting the male/female breakdown of the population and prepare baseline case studies in order to identify and to eliminate unintentional discrimination in delivering goods and services and thereby improve planning of future activities.

11 In its broadest sense, a UNHCR programme or project which mainstreams refugee women should attempt to:

- achieve greater involvement of refugee women both as participants and beneficiaries in the social and economic activities of the project;

- increase their status and participation in the community/society;

- provide a catalyst through which they can have access to better employment, education, services and opportunities in their society;

- take into account the particular social relationship between the refugee women and their families.

Underlying these broad definitions is the assumption that refugee women are participating or should participate at all levels of project and programme development, from the initial identification of resources and needs to the evaluation stage.

IV ORGANIZATIONAL GOALS

12 The organizational goals of UNHCR regarding refugee women are:

a) to provide protection appropriate to their specific needs;

b) to identify an appropriate durable solution;

c) to provide assistance which will encourage the realization of their full potential and encourage their participation in preparing for the durable solution.

V POLICY OBJECTIVES

13 The policy objectives which support the overall organizational goals are:

a) to recognize that refugee women represent, either as single women or with their dependants, approximately 80 per cent of UNHCR's target population and that programmes can be effective only if they are planned with an adequate understanding of, and consultation with, this group;

b) to ensure that the specific protection needs and the legal rights of refugee women are understood and that adequate measures are taken to respond;

c) to support the efforts of refugee women by recognizing their needs and resources and ensuring their participation in UNHCR's protection and assistance activities;

d) to ensure that the differing needs and resources of refugee women and refugee men are considered in programme activities and, where necessary for cultural or social reasons, undertake special efforts to develop specific activities to ensure women benefit equally from programmes;

e) to place particular emphasis on strategies to protect and assist refugee women, recognizing that becoming a refugee can result not only in an unaccustomed social role such as becoming a single head of household or being without extended family support but also in [a] substantially increased physical workload in building and maintaining the future of the entire family;

f) to ensure that refugee women are equitably represented in resettlement programmes;

g) to encourage staff members of UNHCR and implementing partners to ensure that the integration of refugee women's resources/needs takes place in his/her area of competence.

VI OPERATIONAL OBJECTIVES

14 Operational objectives provide the basis for the development of appropriate activities and work plans to support implementation of UNHCR's Policy on Refugee Women. These are:

a) to develop mechanisms to ensure that the resources and needs of refugee women are addressed in all stages of programme (protection and assistance) planning, management and evaluation systems;

b) to co-operate with implementing partners, other United Nations institutions, governments and development agencies with a view to benefiting from their experience in women in development activities and, where appropriate, adapting these to UNHCR's specific programming requirements, sharing with them the long-term development implications specific to the situation of refugee women and appropriate methods of incorporating their specific needs and resources into programming activities;

c) to develop communication strategies to call attention to the situation of refugee women of the public, NGOs, other United Nations agencies, donors, and host countries;

d) to develop specific plans for each organizational work unit within UNHCR which will encourage and facilitate consultation and participation of refugee women, and serve as a means of monitoring and maintaining this consultation and participation;

e) to develop training courses for staff of UNHCR and implementing partners to assist them in identifying opportunities for increased participation of refugee women in their areas of competence;

f) to improve the efficiency and effectiveness of protection and assistance programmes by ensuring that adequate attention is given to the needs and resources of all members of the target population;

g) to review and, where necessary, amend existing policies to ensure that they adequately take into consideration the situation and participation of all members of the target population;

h) to improve data collection and needs assessment in order to have a more accurate representation of the refugee population in order to target programmes more effectively to specific social groups;

i) to ensure that there are adequate female field staff to work with refugee women, and, accordingly, to review staffing and recruitment policies to ensure that there is an equitable representation of female staff and that this is adequately reflected in appointments, posting and promotion activities by UNHCR.

j) to review present operational activities and identify means of improving them in order to facilitate participation of refugee women, and achieve a greater understanding of their needs and resources.●

A FRAMEWORK FOR PEOPLE-ORIENTED PLANNING IN REFUGEE SITUATIONS: A Practical Planning Tool for Refugee Workers
■■■■■■■ Mary B. Anderson and Ann Brazeau

ACKNOWLEDGEMENTS

The Gender Analysis Framework (GAF) on which this paper is based was published in: Overholt, Anderson, Cloud and Austin, eds, *Gender Roles in Development Projects: A Case Book*, Kumarian Press, W. Hartford, CN, 1985. Credit for the concepts, therefore, must go to Catherine A. Overholt, Mary B. Anderson, Kathleen Cloud and James E. Austin. The GAF has been used in training in a number of international agencies, including The World Bank, the US Agency for International Development, the Canadian International Development Agency, the United Nations Population Fund (UNFPA), the Australian International Development Assistance Bureau and others.

In addition 'An Approach to Integrating Development and Programming' (Mary B. Anderson/Peter J. Woodrow) and 'Refugee Participation in Emerency Relief Operations' (F.C. Cuny) formed a basis for much of this paper. Several internal papers produced by UNHCR staff have been extremely useful:

● 'UNHCR Refugee Emergency Alert System' (Draft), L. Druke, January 1990.
● 'Needs and Resources Assessment Checklist' (Draft), R. White, August 1990.
● 'Action on Social and Cultural Issues in Refugee Emergencies', M. Schloeter/ J. Williamson, October 1986.

Many UNHCR staff have provided constructive suggestions and comments in a series of 'brainstorming' sessions, and in their participation in the pilot versions of this training course. Their support is greatly appreciated.

PEOPLE-ORIENTED PLANNING IN REFUGEE SITUATIONS
Background
In 1990, the Executive Committee of the High Commissioner's programme approved a Policy on Refugee Women which basically called for the improvement of participation and access of refugee women in all programmes. This training tool was designed to assist refugee workers in this process by providing them with a frame-

work for analysing the socio-cultural factors in a refugee society which can influence the success of planned activities.

At the end of this training course you will be able to:

- target your programmes more appropriately and, thus, use UNHCR's resources more efficiently;
- ensure that UNHCR programmes do not disadvantage women and girls relative to men and boys, and, even better, that disparities between the sexes may be reduced by UNHCR programmes;
- increase the opportunities for refugees to assume responsibility for their own management and programmes, again making better use of UNHCR's resources.

Introduction

To plan refugee protection and assistance activities efficiently and effectively, refugee workers must analyse the social and economic roles of women and men in the refugee community and understand how these will affect and be affected by planned activities. In the refugee context, these socio-economic roles have been disrupted and are constantly changing through the various stages of the refugee condition, i.e. departure, flight, arrival, asylum, durable solutions. Therefore a major factor in planning for refugees is the concept of change and specifically the implications of these socio-economic role changes to the planning process.

In the long-term refugee situation, a certain stabilization of roles may occur, but even then it can usually be assumed that these roles are different from those of pre-flight and are, therefore, regarded as temporary by the refugees themselves. It is therefore essential in planning activities for refugees that there be an in-depth understanding of the dynamics of change working within the society which will determine to a great extent the acceptance and success of the project. It is also essential to plan consciously towards the expected durable solution. Even though that solution may be voluntary return to the country of origin, the socio-economic situation may have become very different with the passage of time, and returnees must be prepared for this.

Whether you are planning programmes for food distribution, water, sanitation, agriculture, accommodation or health, socio-economic conditions and changes in the community are major factors which will determine the ability of refugees to benefit from and participate in these activities. A knowledge of socio-economic arrangements and the changes in these arrangements will also enable you to build appropriate protection aspects into all of your planned assistance activities.

Refugee participation is also a major factor in determining whether or not the project will be successful. Failure to involve refugees will ultimately lead to several consequences:
- increasing lethargy on the part of refugees;
- cost increases;
- decrease in communication.[1]

At the earliest stage of a refugee emergency a preliminary socio-economic and demographic assessment of the population must be taken in order to ensure that assumptions for future planning are basically correct. 'Fine-tuning' can occur at a later stage.

It is important to note if the overall population profile has been distorted by the refugee situation. Who are the refugees? Has the typical profile been maintained? Are they mostly young men? Mostly children? Mostly male or female single heads of household? In a refugee situation when men are killed in conflict, adolescent boys flee to avoid conscription, or women and children evacuate regions of fighting, population profiles change. Such major demographic distortions have to be taken into consideration and adaptations made in traditional delivery of programmes because people in refugee populations are also having to assume new and demanding roles in their society.

It is most important to ensure that socio-economic factors are included in initial planning in order to avoid cutting some refugees off unintentionally from the benefits of the planned programmes because their specific and changed roles do not give them the time or physical ability to participate. This is often the case for female refugees, who for cultural reasons are often neither encouraged nor are able to participate in planning of activities for which they are the primary beneficiaries (house construction, water and sanitation systems, adult literacy, food preparation, etc.). A note of caution here: do not make assumptions based on your own 'stereotypes' of the culture. Because the society is in transition, traditional roles may no longer apply. Find out from the refugees, both men and women, how these roles have changed, and are changing.

The three-step framework which follows is intended as a tool for planners of refugee programmes. It can be adapted to the level of detail required by any particular situation and is intended as a 'map' of the direction to take in analysing the refugee population, with a view to a clear definition of the needs and resources of the various members of the refugee population.

After you have read the 'map' or Analytic Framework, which forms the basis of this planning tool, you will be introduced to a case study which will illustrate how the framework can be used in a typical refugee situation and what the implications are for good planning. A socio-economic and demographic analysis is only one component of project planning. However, it is a critical one, particularly since we aim to prepare refugees for a future solution where they are independent and self-reliant.

After the case study, the course animator will illustrate people-oriented planning with examples from your daily work. These may include UNHCR documents such as:

- Technical mission, emergency, repatriation, reports;
- Project Descriptions;
- Project Monitoring Reports;
- Evaluation Reports;
- Statements of Field Objectives;
- or any others you suggest.

ANALYTICAL FRAMEWORK

The People-orientated Analytical Framework has three components:
1. Activities Analysis.
2. Access and Control of Resources Analysis.
3. Determinants Analysis.

Activities Analysis

The basic female/male division of social and economic roles and responsibilities is disrupted when people become refugees. It is therefore essential to know what people were doing before and what they are doing or are able to do now in the refugee situation for which you are planning (entry, first asylum, durable solutions).

Protection is an important activity which must be highlighted here. Protection activities are integral to all assistance activities. UNHCR is responsible for the protection of refugees because they are no longer able or willing to avail themselves of the legal protection of their country of origin.

For returning populations UNHCR monitors the guarantees and assurances which form the basis for the decision to return. In addition to legal protection, there is a 'protection hierarchy' in the community. Typically, this may involve communities (families, tribes, social groupings) protecting individuals; men protecting women; adults protecting children; people in the prime of life protecting the elderly. In some societies, older women protect younger women; married women protect unmarried women; menopausal women protect fertile women. Such protection may be legal, physical (through strength or the threat of strength) or social (accomplished through chaperonage). Because such patterns are often disrupted by the changes which occur when people leave their homes, these are important factors to consider when planning refugee assistance programmes, in order to ensure that these activities include the protection factor. For example, identifying specific activities for unaccompanied children, providing special accommodation for single women, or ensuring that supply distribution schemes do not contribute to exploitation of these 'unprotected' groups is easier if you have identified protection 'gaps' which occur because of changes in the population profile and in people's roles and responsibilities.

Specifically, you ask the following questions for the pre-refugee setting:

What did they do?

- this includes production of goods and services such as farming, domestic work, teaching, business activities, etc;
- it also includes household production – house-building, household production, such as meal preparation, fuel collection, home gardening, food preservation, etc;
- and it includes social, political and religious activities which in some cultures take considerable resources, such as traditional ceremonies, community meetings, etc.

Who did what?

Is this activity usually carried out by men? by women? or both? by children? by elders? It is important to note that tasks within each overall activity must be specified to reflect the responsibilities within the society. For example in agriculture, men may be responsible for land clearance, women and children for seeding and weeding, men for harvesting, women for preservation and sale of products, etc. Knowing this type of information will assist you, for example, in targeting agricultural extension training and distribution of seeds and tools.

Where and when did they do it?

- this helps you to judge the time use and mobility of the refugees.
- you ask: what was the frequency of the activity? (once a day, every week, etc.), how long did it take? (all day, all morning, evenings, etc.), where it took place? in the home, in the village, on agricultural land, etc.

Understanding when a particular task is done and how long it takes is one way of understanding time constraints and opportunities for different people in the community. For example, if men in an agricultural society are responsible for land preparation while women carry out the planting and cultivation tasks, one can determine who will be fully occupied at which seasons and who might have unallocated time. Or, if a technology is introduced that shortens the time required to collect water, and young girls have typically been responsible for water collection, then one may find that more girls are allowed by their families to attend school. When some people are responsible for tasks that occur regularly (such as women involved in household production), while others are responsible for tasks that occur seasonally (such as men involved in land preparation and harvesting of crops), the impact on their time of any project intervention may differ greatly.

What resources were used?

This includes tangible resources such as money, land, tools, housing, animals, etc. and 'invisible' resources such as education, skills, labour, community support. We ask which resources were used to accomplish the tasks in the pre-refugee setting for two reasons. First, some resources, such as land, cannot be moved so that when farmers become refugees, they lose their basic productive resource unless the host country is willing to provide it. Other resources, such as skills (for example, teaching or trading), are portable and can continue to provide a livelihood even in a refugee setting. If women were farmers and men had other transferable skills, the

loss of resources for production would be greater for women in the refugee setting than for men. Or, if water is a resource in household production, and it is provided closer to the living quarters in a refugee setting than in the pre-refugee home, the time required for accomplishing the activity of water collection is lessened. Since time can also be viewed as a resource, the provision of one resource (water) increases another (time), but only for those individuals (male or female) whose responsibility it was to collect the water.

Having addressed the above four questions for the pre-refugee setting you ask the same questions for the situation for which you are planning. If you are planning a repatriation activity for example, you would look at the present activities of the refugees and then at the socio-economic activities in the home country with a view to identifying differences which could have an influence on effective reintegration. We have pointed out earlier

---

ACTIVITIES ANALYSIS
(complete for both pre-refugee and in the present situation)

Activities	Who	Where	When/How long	Resources used
1. Protection				
2. Production of goods				
e.g. carpentry				
farming				
3. and services				
e.g. teaching				
domestic labour				
4. Household production				
e.g. childcare				
home garden				
water collection				
5. Social/political/religious				
e.g. community meeting				
ceremonies				

that the refugee society is in transition. The society to which refugees will return may also have changed considerably or not changed at all, with the result that new roles assumed by returnees may not be compatible with those in their former home.

At the end of this activities analysis you should have a good idea of how the traditional activities of women and men have been affected by becoming a refugee; who has more or less time to devote to project activities; and some indication as to when and where to plan activities so that your target population can realistically participate. Also you will have a good idea of the 'gaps' in activities which can be used to identify appropriate interventions and at what time to plan them in the refugee setting.

The form on p.116 shows the Activities Analysis.

Analysis of resource use and control

In the next stage of analysis you should look at what resources refugees controlled and used before they became refugees and what resources they control and use now. You will recall that we listed 'resources' in Table 1 and that these included material resources such as money, animals, land, housing, tools, etc. and invisible resources such as education, income-generating skills, cultural ties, time, labour, etc. We make the distinction between 'use' and 'control' because it will have a direct bearing or the refugees' ability to take charge of their situation.

Refugees may have owned and therefore 'controlled' land before flight; afterwards they may use land controlled by others. In a returnee situation, people may have lost their land rights in their country of origin and be unable to use newly acquired non-agricultural skills. In the pre-refugee setting, men may have controlled family

income because they were employed outside the home while women had the use of it. Therefore it would likely have been the men who determined household spending priorities. In the refuge setting the men may no longer have a source of income or they may be absent fighting or have been killed in conflict. Therefore control of family resources will have to be assumed entirely by or shared with women family members who will require new skills. These factors are important to know if you are planning income-generating activities for example.

The example overleaf shows a chart for recording and analysing information about female and male control and use of resources. Men and women will have lost different resources, they will possess different skills and knowledge, and the resources they will receive will differ depending on how and to whom they are provided.

At the end of this analysis you will have a clear understanding of what resources have been lost, what have been acquired, who is better or worse off in the refugee setting (men, women, old/young), and whose activities have been most affected by resource shifts. This will help you identify which parts of the population need most protection and assistance, the type of protection and assistance they require, and what priorities should be assigned to your proposed interventions. With this information you can ensure that your planned activities do not further disadvantage a group which has already suffered disproportionate losses of resources in the refugee situation. If you are planning a repatriation programme you will look at the resource situation among the refugees in the country of asylum and the likely resources available in the country to which the refugees are returning. The 'gaps' will indicate to you where to plan your assis-

RESOURCE USE AND CONTROL

Lost Resource	Who Used (men/women)	Who Controlled
labour		
legal rights		
Land		
Shelter		
Tools		
schools		
health care		
income		

Brought by Refugees Resource	Who has (men/women)	Who Uses
1. Skills		
e.g. political		
manufacturing		
carpentry		
sewing		
cleaning		
agricultural		
2. Knowledge		
e.g. literacy		
teaching		
medicine/health		

Provided to refugees Resources	To whom (male heads/household) (female heads/household)	How
Food		
Shelter		
Clothing		
Education		
Legal services		
Health		

tance. The resource profile also helps you identify the resources which do exist in the refugee community. At all times your aim should be to build on these existing resources in order to encourage self-reliance.

Determinants analysis:

A final stage in the analytical 'map' is to look at determinants. These are the external factors which determine or influence the roles and responsibilities, and the resource use of women and men and which, therefore, can affect the outcome of your planned activities. They are broad and interrelated and include such factors as:

(a) general economic conditions, such as poverty levels, inflation rates, income distribution, international terms of trade, infrastructure;

(b) institutional structures, including the nature of government bureaucracies and arrangements for the generation and dissemination of knowledge, technology, and skills;

(c) demographic factors;

(d) community norms and social hierarchy, such as family/community power structure and religious beliefs. These can be particularly important among refugee groups where women's and men's roles are changing;

(e) legal parameters;

(f) training and education;

(g) political events, both internal and external;

(h) national attitude to refugees; and

(i) attitude of refugees to development/assistance workers

We do not provide a table for this analysis because the purpose of identifying these 'determinants' is to consider which ones affect activities or resources and how they affect them. This helps you identify external constraints and opportunities that you should consider in planning your programmes. It will help you anticipate and better predict the inputs of your programmes.

CONCLUSION

Tools are only instruments which are used by people. It is people who have the skills, experience, knowledge, plans and vision who put tools to good, or poor, use. The People-oriented Planning Framework is a tool which facilitates programme and project planning, implementation and evaluation. It alerts refugee workers to variables of which we must be aware and it reminds us that the refugees are active, productive and resourceful people rather than merely passive victims of a disaster. It, further, reminds us that women, as well as men, are active producers in the economy and society and that one critical variable in programme planning is change in the gender division of roles, responsibilities and resources. The Framework also provides a structure for organizing information so that relationships among factors (between men, women, boys and girls; between activities in the economic and social spheres; between activities and resources which are used to perform them; between larger forces and local, social and economic arrangements) are highlighted. The tool does not, itself, give answers about which programmes are best. It does provide insights which, when used appropriately, can improve the efficiency and effectiveness of international assistance provided to refugees.●

DRAFT REPORT OF THE EXPERT GROUP MEETING ON REFUGEE AND DISPLACED WOMEN AND CHILDREN
Vienna, 2–6 July 1990

I. POLICY FRAMEWORK

1. The Expert Group on refugee and displaced women and children recognizing the fundamental equality of refugee and displaced women and men and the necessity for women's full participation and empowerment in the development of their potential for self-sufficiency, urges that:

   a. the civil, political, economic, social and cultural rights of refugee and displaced women and children be reaffirmed by the international community, with due regard to relevant international universal and regional legal instruments, including the Convention on the Elimination of All Forms of Discrimination Against Women, the Convention on the Rights of Children, the 1951 Convention and its 1967 Protocol relating to the status of refugees, the 1949 Geneva Conventions, and the two 1977 additional Protocols;

   b. the root causes of refugee and related situations and their solutions be addressed in an urgent manner at the national, regional and international levels; and

   c. all governments that have not yet done so, ratify or accede to and implement the relevant international instruments related to refugees and humanitarian law.

2. The Expert Group urges implementation of the 1990 ECOSOC resolution 34/2 calling on Governments, relevant UN agencies, and concerned non-governmental organizations to 'increase their efforts to respond to the specific needs of refugee women, in particular those of long-term refugees, as well as displaced women, in the areas of education, health, physical safety, social services, skills training, employment and income generating activities, and to involve refugee women in the planning and implementation of such programme'. (E/CN.6/1990/1, 6 April 1990)

II. COMPONENTS OF POLICIES

3. Relevant UN and other international and regional organizations, host governments, non-governmental organizations and funding agencies which play a role in the protection of and/or assistance to refugees should be encouraged to develop a policy statement on refugee women and children, including a time frame for implementation. This policy statement should provide for the full integration of the concern for refugee women and children into every aspect of that agency's mandate and programmes.

   a. Assistance and protection efforts should be built upon a realistic assessment of the resources, capabilities, needs and priorities of refugee women and children. Appropriate accountability and monitoring procedures should be introduced to ensure that programmes proposed by organizations address these issues and ensure that refugee women and children have equal access to the services which will be provided.

   b. Assistance and protection activities can only be truly effective if refugee women themselves are full and active partners in the process of assessing needs, planning and implementing programmes.

   c. The international community, in its concerted response to refugee situations, should give priority to extending international protection to refugee women and children, and to seeking appropriate durable solutions to their problems. Moreover, the close link between protection and assistance measures requires that protection concerns be borne in mind when planning and implementing assistance programmes.

d. Refugee women and children must be protected from physical violence, sexual abuse, abduction and those circumstances which force them into prostitution and/or other illegal activities.

e. Given the need for durable solutions for refugee women and children, all assistance from the outset of a refugee emergency should build on capacities and resources of refugee women and lead to long-term self-reliance.

f. Refugee women and children are affected to a greater extent than men by displacement. The international community should further strengthen its efforts to address the problems and causes contributing to the displacement and to the outflow of asylum seekers, as well as measures that encourage voluntary repatriation and local reintegration.

g. Access to affected refugee populations should be ensured so that assistance and protection can reach refugees, particularly refugee women and children, in need of such programmes.

h. UN agencies, national government agencies and NGOs that have a proven capacity to design and implement projects for women and children should be involved in programming for refugees.

i. The international community should more effectively target assistance to refugee-affected areas of host countries, with particular focus on the most vulnerable populations in these areas.

j. In the promotion of voluntary repatriation and local integration, information should be directed in particular to refugee women.

k. National, regional and international agencies should collect and analyse data on refugees, returnees and displaced persons, with a particular focus on gender disaggregation.

l. Gender-sensitive women should be recruited and advanced to management and field positions in international organizations, national governments and NGOs in order to provide appropriate assistance to refugee women. Key staff of organizations working with refugees should receive gender impact awareness training.

4. UNHCR, UNRWA and other relevant organizations should utilize every conceivable strategy to increase their resource pool in order to enhance their ability to cover the entire range of refugee needs, with particular attention to those contributing to the well-being of refugee women and children.

III. RECOMMENDATIONS
Protection of refugee women and children

5. Refugees themselves should be invited to provide support for improving the protection of refugee women and of refugee children. The establishment of women's associations should be encouraged, as should that of refugee committees, which should include refugee women.

6. The staff of relevant organizations and authorities, including local military and law-enforcement agencies should be

made fully aware of the rights and needs of refugee women and children.

7. Refugee women and children should be informed about their rights and entitlements.

8. Greater input from refugee women is required in developing mechanisms to improve the reporting of physical and sexual abuse, establishing preventive measures and planning and implementing corresponding assistance and other programmes.

9. As appropriate, relevant organizations and host governments should increase their female field protection and assistance staff with a specific task of assisting in identifying and providing support for refugee women and children who are maybe the victims of physical violence and sexual abuse. Host governments and other relevant authorities should ensure that such staff have direct and unhindered access to refugee women and children.

10. The presence of qualified personnel, in particular international staff, of relevant organizations should be strengthened along escape routes, in reception centres, camps and settlements and in other areas where refugee women and refugee children find themselves in order to assist in providing greater protection for the affected populations, and to monitor and report regularly on the situation.

11. Physical security of refugee women and children should be ensured in camps and settlements.

12. Military or armed attacks on refugee camps and settlements should be prohibited.

13. Host governments and other relevant authorities should undertake special law enforcement measures in order to ensure that persons who have committed crimes against refugee women and children are prosecuted.

14. Refugee women and children who are the victims of violence should be addressed as a matter of protection priority through professional, cultural, as well as gender based appropriate counselling and other services.

15. Women who claim refugee status should have full and equal access to refugee status determination procedures and be appropriately assisted to present their claim in the hearing process.

16. Individual identification/registration documents should be issued to all refugee and returnee women and, whenever possible children, whether their refugee status has been determined individually or as part of a group in a mass influx situation. Such documents should be issued irrespective of whether the women and children are accompanied by male family members.

17. Training should be provided to sensitize those responsible for interviewing and assessing the claims of women asylum-seekers.

18. Governments are encouraged to adopt and implement Women-at-Risk programmes to resettle those refugee women who are in critical conditions, and who may not otherwise meet existing admissibility criteria.

Protection of refugee children (children-specific recommendations)

19. The life and physical well-being of refugee children should be given the highest priority. The children should be protected against all types of aggression, including physical violence and sexual abuse.

20. All parties should participate in advocacy efforts at international and national levels to assure the rights of

children including refugee and displaced children for survival, protection
and development by promoting a
'child first' ethos and the idea for 'children as a zone of peace'.

21. In every refugee and displaced emergency a recognized 'child advocate'
should be designated by appropriate
international organizations to advocate
for the protection and well-being of
children including, but not limited to,
children who are unaccompanied, sub-
jected to recruitment, abused, impris-
oned, detained or coerced into practices
that violate their cultures or beliefs.

22. Recruitment of refugee and displaced
children into armed forces and armed
groups should be vigorously de-
nounced and all necessary steps take
to end this practice.

23. Special provisions should be implemented for the determination of
refugee status for unaccompanied
minors, keeping in mind that decisions
must be made based on the best interest of the child.

24. Appropriate accommodation should be
provided to children to ensure their
safety, well-being and physical and
mental health during the period of status determination.

25. Given the increasing numbers of
undocumented and stateless children,
special initiatives must be taken and
more effective procedures developed
to obtain nationality as well as changing
national laws that cause statelessness.

Protection of displaced women and children.

26. Greater recognition and designation
must be made with respect to the
plight of displaced persons. Since most
of the protection problems faced by
refugee women and children are common to those of displaced women and
children, national governments and

the international community should
address this issue as a matter of urgency, taking into account the relevant
provisions of the 1949 Geneva
Conventions and the two 1977
Additional Protocols.

27. In this regard, governments are urged
to respect and implement relevant
international humanitarian and other
legal instruments, as well as appropriate regional national instruments.

28. National governments are also urged
to ensure the provision of protection
and assistance to displaced women
and children, while in places of temporary residence until such time as an
appropriate solution is found, and to
assess the need for additional international instruments to address those
protection concerns.

29. The mandates of the international
organizations to address the needs of
displaced women and children should
be examined, clarified and strengthened as needed.

Assistance to refugee and displaced women

1. FOOD DISTRIBUTION

30. To combat malnutrition and increase
self-reliance, refugee and displaced
women should have the opportunity to
produce, trade or otherwise acquire food.
To the extent that food assistance continues to be needed, women must play
key leadership roles in its distribution.

2. NUTRITION

31. Food rations must be nutritionally balanced, have adequate caloric content
and be consistent with traditional
dietary practices. Special attention
must be paid to the needs of children,
women of child-bearing age, and the
elderly.

32. WFP and other donors of food aid
should be encouraged to fortify food

aid with needed vitamins and minerals.

33. Systems for monitoring the nutritional status of all refugee and displaced women and children should be established. Refugee and displaced women should be trained to monitor the nutritional status and that of their children. Where nutritional deficiencies or declining nutritional status is detected, immediate steps should be taken to improve the nutritional contents of the rations.

34. Programmes to educate refugee and displaced women regarding nutrition should be established or strengthened as needed.

3. HEALTH

35. Refugee and displaced women should participate fully in the design and implementation of all refugee health programmes. These should emphasize primary health care and be community based. Women home visitor and traditional birth attendant (TBA) programmes should be included.

36. Institutions operating health programmes for refugee and displaced persons should be urged to set staffing guidelines under which at least 50 per cent of their workers would be women. Increased efforts should be made to identify and train women, including refugee and displaced women, as health workers.

37. Immunization, maternal and child health services, including gynaecological services, education regarding sexually transmitted diseases and harmful traditional practices, and family planning education services should be available, as well as rehabilitation programmes for disabled women and children.

38. Counselling and mental health services should be available, particularly for victims of torture, rape and other sexual abuse, trauma and physical violence.

4. WATER

39. All refugee and displaced women and children should have access to safe drinking water and sanitary facilities, taking into account the special situation of uprooted women.

40. Refugee and displaced women should be involved in the identification of requirements and preferences concerning the type and location of water points and should be trained in the use and maintenance.

41. Culturally appropriate resources must be made to enable women to collect water, bathe and wash clothing.

5. SHELTER

42. Refugee and displaced women must be consulted as to their needs and priorities in the development of any site plan or housing/community infrastructure.

43. Plans for placement and construction of housing should provide for as much long-term security as possible and facilitate the daily task of refugee and displaced women.

44. Refugee and displaced women should be involved in maintenance and improvement of existing community facilities.

45. In urban areas, the allowance provided for housing should be sufficient to provide safe housing, and whenever possible, should be issued to the female adult in the household.

6. ADULT EDUCATION, EMPLOYMENT AND INCOME GENERATION

46. Refugee and displaced women should be included in the planning and implementation of skills training, employment and income-generating

programmes for the whole refugee community. Special programmes for women may sometimes be necessary for cultural reasons.

47. Scholarship schemes should ensure equitable participation of refugee and displaced women.

48. Certificates should be provided for formal and non-formal education, so that these qualifications can be recognized in countries of asylum, origin, integration and/or resettlement.

49. Training programmes should be promoted with the objective of providing refugee and displaced women with marketable and business skills in traditional and non-traditional activities, including skills training in agricultural and non-agricultural activities, functional literacy and numeracy, leadership and managerial training.

50. Viable and sustainable employment creation schemes and income generating activities should be designed and implemented on the basis of sound needs assessment, research and feasibility studies, with the full participation of refugee and displaced women. Projects should be assessed to determine their impact.

51. Host governments should be encouraged to issue work permits and other relevant documents to refugee women.

52. Support and assistance should be given to refugee and displaced women to form associations of their own choosing, including promotion of informal and formal organizations and co-operatives.

53. The capacity and information sharing of organizations involved in employment and income-generating activities for refugee and displaced persons should be improved.

54. To the extent possible, host governments and other relevant authorities should be encouraged to provide refugee and displaced women opportunities for productive activities, including access to land that is at least sufficient for household gardening and animal husbandry.

7. LONG-TERM SOLUTIONS

55. Whenever repatriation, local integration and resettlement are possible, refugee women should participate in planning assistance and rehabilitation programmes and should be provided with adequate information to make decisions on their own futures.

8. DATA GATHERING

56. The responsible government agencies and UN should compile statistics and demographic profiles of the refugee and displaced population which highlight information about gender, age, household composition, education, skills status and other relevant information. In addition, information should be collected on the general impact of the uprooting experience on these women, including a full assessment of the various activities for which they are responsible.

57. Gender-delineated statistics must be collected to determine the number of women and children utilizing programmes in all spheres affecting the life of refugee and displaced persons: education, training, employment, health care, etc.

58. All assistance programmes should have a monitoring and self-evaluation component. When necessary, training in programme evaluation should be provided to programme implementation. In addition, responsible governments and UN agencies should regularly evaluate programmes to ensure the quality of the services and the access

of refugee and displaced women to them.

59. Research should be conducted on such urgent issues as the needs of refugee women and children upon repatriation, given the potential for the return of millions of refugees, and the situation of internally displaced women.

Assistance to refugee children — children-specific recommendations

1. SURVIVAL

60. All parties should join in actions to achieve the survival and well-being of women and children through attainment of the child survival and development goals for the 1990s, with special efforts to ensure that refugee and displaced children and mothers are included therein, for instance:

   a. Strengthening efforts for the immunization of refugee and displaced children against the six immunizable diseases as a part of the global thrust to achieve universal child immunization and sustaining that coverage in the future.

   b. Strengthening efforts for the universal immunization of refugee and displaced mothers with tetanus toxoid and sustaining coverage.

   c. Education of all refugee and displaced mothers on the use of oral rehydration therapy and ensuring its proper use to combat diarrhoeal dehydration.

   d. Training and employing adequate numbers of primary health care workers, including traditional birth attendants (TBAs), is necessary to ensure that basic prenatal and postnatal care and safe birth delivery methods is provided to refugee and displaced women.

   e. Establishing systems of monitoring the nutritional status of all refugee and displaced children and ensuring actions against nutritional deficien-

cies through appropriate programme interventions. Where nutritional deficiencies or declining nutritional status is detected, immediate interventions should be taken.

   f. Traditional diets and food preparation practices should be taken into consideration whenever possible.

   g. That all refugee and displaced persons have access to safe drinking water and sanitary facilities, taking into consideration the special needs of children.

61. Persons with special responsibility for the well-being of children should be part of every emergency programme.

2. EDUCATION AND SKILLS TRAINING

62. Goverments and international organizations should take immediate steps to ensure that all refugee and displaced children have access to basic education.

63. Female and male refugees and displaced should have equal access to education programmes.

64. Such education programmes should be adapted to the needs of the refugee population including instruction in the mother language.

65. In such situations where the formal school system fails or is unable to provide school opportunities to refugee and displaced children, alternative methods of coping must be found to ensure the rights of children to attain basic and primary education.

66. Governments, international organizations and the NGO community should provide skills and vocational training to refugee and displaced children to enhance their development and provide basic life skills.

67. Particular efforts must be made to sensitize male refugee and displaced leaders to the need for education for

female children.

68. Governments and other authorities should make every effort to ensure continuity of the education systems established for refugees and displaced persons.

3. CHILDREN IN SITUATIONS OF ARMED CONFLICT

69. Support should be provided to expand the level of humanitarian aid to children in conflict situations particularly those displaced within their own country by building upon and expanding the successful work carried out in this regard by international, governmental and non-governmental organizations.

4. CHILDREN WITH SPECIAL NEEDS

70. *Unaccompanied Children:* Special efforts should be taken to ensure that the care and protection of unaccompanied children is guaranteed, including where necessary, the following actions: identification, documentation, ensuring basic services, family tracing and where possible family reunification, assigning a legal advocate, and ensuring adequate care arrangements on an emergency, interim and permanent basis.

71. *Disabled Children:* Special efforts should be taken to ensure that disabled children receive assistance that will enable them to participate to the extent possible as full members of society.

72. *Female Children:* Special emphasis should be given to ensure that female children have equal access to all services and opportunities.

73. *Traumatized Children:* Refugee and displaced children who are suffering from trauma should be provided counselling and mental health services particularly if those are victims of torture, rape and other physical and sexual abuse.

IV. ORGANIZATIONAL MATTERS
Summary of statements

74. The Director of the Division for the Advancement of Women opened the meeting. In her statement, she emphasized that the meeting was concerned with finding solutions for the situation of refugee and displaced women and children, a problem that was as old as humanity. She reported that the current estimate of the refugee population in the world today was approximately 14 million of which women and children represented the majority. The joint responsibility for finding solutions to the problem was reflected in the participation at the meeting of host countries, donor countries, international agencies and non-governmental organizations. Also present were experts and refugees who would be able to report on their experiences. She stated that it was vital to apply gender-tests to the questions raised and the recommendations formulated to ensure that the issue of refugee women as opposed to the refugee population in general was addressed. The format of the meeting was such that the 'life cycle' of refugee women was covered, with emphasis on protection in the initial stages of displacement, on assistance in camps or other settlements and the identificaton of durable solutions. The meeting was concerned with both refugee and displaced women and children and, although the groups shared many of the same problems, it was to be borne in mind that they had different legal status.

75. The Director elaborated on the specific problems that women and children specifically encounter during flight and resettlement, such as sexual abuse, diversion of food and medical supplies and dramatic changes in social status.

She stated that, although the 1951 Convention on refugees and its 1967 protocol were intended to be gender-neutral, discrimination could occur in their interpretation. Together with the women in the host countries, refugee women were often discriminated against and were not aware of their legal rights. The Director noted that refugee status was often of long duration, and not a temporary status as was often believed, caused by the continuation of the conditions in the country of origin that had caused the initial flight. She drew attention to the increased burden on countries of refuge which in themselves were often developing countries with limited resources and identified voluntary repatriation or settlement in a third country as possible solutions.

76. The Director stressed that the focus when looking at the problems of refugee women should be that they are a great resource and should be encouraged to participate actively in decision-making and management of their communities and given the tools and power to enhance their social integration and their security. She concluded that the meeting would hopefully produce recommendations for the action needed to improve the fortunes of the millions of refugee and displaced women and children and the ways to carry out that action, including the necessary commitments and resource provision.

77. The Senior Coordinator for Refugee Women for the Office of the United Nations High Commissioner for Refugees (UNHCR) reported that, in its fortieth year of protecting and assisting refugees, the provision of protection, food, clothing, shelter and water had become increasingly the sole focus of their programmes. Assistance activities were in serious jeopardy due to budget constraints. This would mean that thousands of refugee children would not have access to even primary education, that thousands of refugee women and children would not have the benefit of basic counselling which would assist them in leading productive lives following the trauma of flight, and that many refugee women would not have access to functional literacy and income-generating activities which would provide them with the skills to prepare them for self-reliance. She stated that most of the people who would suffer from UNHCR's budget cuts would be women and children, as they represented between 70 and 80 per cent of the beneficiaries of the programmes. UNHCR had developed gender impact training for staff and implementing partners and their procedures manual and reporting process required that the specific situation of refugee women be addressed. She expressed the hope that the meeting would make concrete recommendations to the Commission on the Status of Women in 1991 which would encourage the international community to mobilize both its resources and those of refugee women as partners in building towards the future.

Attendance

79. The expert group meeting was attended by one consultant, government representatives, experts, intergovernmental organizations, organizations and agencies of the United Nations system, non-governmental organizations and research institutes.●

---

[1]Frederick C. Cuny, 'Refugee Participation in Emergency Relief Operations', Refugee Policy Group.

ANNEX III
LIST OF INTERNATIONAL ORGANIZATIONS

International Catholic Migration Commission (ICMC), 37-39 rue de Vermont, 1202 Geneva, tel: 733.41.50, fax: 734.79.29.
President: Mr Edward De Brandt; Vice-President: H.E. Archbishop Pedro Rubiano Saenz; General Secretary: Dr André N. Van Chau.

International Committee of the Red Cross (ICRC), 17 avenue de la Paix, 1202 Geneva, tel: 734.60.01, fax: 733.20.57, telex: 414.226.
President: Cornelio Sommaruga.

International Council of Voluntary Agencies (ICVA), 13 rue Gautier, 1201 Geneva, tel: 732.66.00, fax: 738.99.04, telex: 412586.

Executive Director: Delmar Blasco.
International Organization for Migration (IOM, formerly ICM), 17 route des Morillons, PO Box 71, 1211 Geneva 19, tel: 717.91.11, fax: 798.61.50. Director General: James N. Purcell.

League of Red Cross and Red Crescent Societies, 17 chemin des Crets, PO Box 372, 1211 Geneva 19, tel: 734.55.80, fax: 733.03.95, telex: 22555. Secretary-General: Pär Stenbäck.

Lutheran World Federation (LWF), Lutheran Center, 390 Park Avenue South, New York, NY 10016, tel: 532.63.50, telex: 4900006094. LRS

NGO Working Group on Refugee Women, Secretariat, Norwegian Refugee Council, Pilestredet 15 B, Oslo 1, N-0164, tel: 11.65.00, fax: 11.65.01, telex: 72343.
Co-ordinator: Eleanor Brenna.

Office of the United Nations High Commissioner for Refugees, Case postale 2500, 1211 Genève 2 Dépôt, tel: 739.81.11, fax: 731.95.46, telex: 41.57.40. High Commissioner: Sadako Ogata.

United Nations Children's Fund (UNICEF), 3 UN Plaza, New York, NY 10017, tel: (212) 326.70.00. Executive Director: James Grant.

United Nations Disaster Relief Co-ordinator (UNDRO), Palais des Nations, CH-1211 Geneva 100, Switzerland, tel: 734.60.11, telex: 28148.

United Nations Relief and Works Agency for Palestine Refugees in the Near East (UNRWA), Vienna International Centre, PO Box 700, A-1400 Vienna, Austria, tel: 431.21131, ext. 4530. Commissioner-General: Ilter Turkmen

World Council of Churches, Commission on Inter-Church Aid, Refugee & World Service, PO Box 2100, 1211 Geneva 2, Switzerland, tel: 791.61.11, fax: 791.03.61, telex: 415 730 oik ch.
Co-ordinator: Melaku Kifle.

World Food Programme (WFP), Via Cristoforo Colombo 426, 00145 Rome, Italy, tel: 06-57971, telex: 626675 WFP 1. Director: Catherine A. Bertini.

---

* For relevant national organizations, please contact the Secretariat of the NGO Working Group on Refugee Women (as above) or the UNHCR Branch Office in your country.

SELECTIVE BIBLIOGRAPHY

African Training and Research Centre for Women (1986) *Refugee and Displaced Women in Independent African States*, Addis Ababa: Economic Commission for Africa.

Agger, Inger (1989) 'Sexual Torture of Political Prisoners: An Overview', *Journal of Traumatic Stress*, Vol. 2, No. 3.

Aitchison, Roberta (1984) 'Reluctant Witnesses', *Cultural Survival Quarterly*, Vol. 8, No. 2, Summer.

Amnesty International (1991) *Women in the Front Line: Human Rights Violations Against Women*, New York: Amnesty International Publications.

Anderson, Mary B. and Peter J. Woodrow (1989) *Rising from the Ashes: Development Strategies in Times of Disaster*, Boulder and San Francisco: Westview Press.

Austrian Relief Committee, *Annual Reports*, 1985–86.

Billard, Annick (1983) 'Women and Health in Afghan Refugee Camps', *Refugees*, Vol. 2.

Boesen, Inger and Ken Pedersen (1988) *Refugee Women in Denmark: Towards a New Identity?* Copenhagen: Danish Refugee Council.

Caplan, Nathan, *et al.* (1985) *Southeast Asian Self-Sufficiency Study: Final Report*. Ann Arbor, Michigan: Institute for Social Research.

Chambers, Robert (1986) 'Hidden Losers? The Impact of Rural Refugees and Refugee Programs on Poorer Hosts', *International Migration Review*, Vol. 20, No. 2.

Clark, Lance (1989) 'Internal Refugees: The Hidden Half', *World Refugee Survey - 1988 in Review*, Washington, DC: US Committee for Refugees.

———— (1987a) 'Refugee Participation: Changing Talk into Action', Washington, DC: Refugee Policy Group.

———— (1987b) 'Refugee Participation Case Study: The Shaba Settlements in Zaire', Washington, DC: Refugee Policy Group.

Cohen, Roberta (1990) 'Human Rights at the UN: Internally Displaced People Need Human Rights Protection', New York: International League for Human Rights.

Connor, Kerry M. (1988) 'Skill Inventory of Afghan Women Refugees in the North West Frontier and Baluchistan Provinces', Islamabad: UNICEF.

Cuny, Fred C. (1987) 'Refugee Participation in Emergency Relief Operations', Washington, DC: Refugee Policy Group.

Dupree, Nancy Hatch (1988). 'The Role of Afghan Women After Repatriation'. Writers' Union for a Free Afghanistan, Peshawar.

Dutch Ministry of Social Affairs and Labour (1984) *Sexual Violence Against Women Refugees*, The Hague: Dutch Ministry of Social Affairs and Labour.

Ferris, Elizabeth (1990) 'Refugee Women and Violence', Geneva: World Council of Churches.

Forbes, Susan (1985) Adaptation and Integration of Recent Refugees in the United States', Washington, DC: Refugee Policy Group.

Forbes Martin, Susan and Emily Copeland (1987), *Making Ends Meet? Refugee Women and Income Generation* (Washington, D.C.: Refugee Policy Group).

Giacaman, Rita (1989) 'Palestinian Women in the Uprising: From Followers to Leaders', *Journal of Refugee Studies*, Vol. 2, No. 1.

Gozdziak, Elzbieta (1988) 'Older Refugees in the United States: From Dignity to Despair', Washington, DC: Refugee Policy Group.

Hall, Eve (1988) *Vocational Training for Women Refugees in Africa: Guidelines from Selected Field Projects*, Training Policies Discussion Paper No. 26, International Labour Organisation, Geneva.

Johnsson, Anders (1988) 'The International

Protection of Women Refugees', paper presented at the International Consultation on Refugee Women, Geneva.

Kelly, Ninette (1989) *Working With Refugee Women: A Practical Guide*, Geneva International NGO Working Group on Refugee Women.

Krill, Francoise (1985) *The Protection of Women in International Humanitarian Law*, Geneva: International Committee of the Red Cross.

Krummel, Sharon (nd) 'Refugee Women and the Experience of Cultural Uprooting', Geneva: Refugee Service, World Council of Churches.

Lawyers Committee for Human Rights (1987) *Seeking Shelter: Cambodians in Thailand*, New York: Lawyers Committee for Human Rights.

Lewin/ICF and Refugee Policy Group (1990) *Promoting Mental Health Services for Refugees: A Handbook on Model Practices*, Washington, DC: Lewin/ICF.

Lie, Suzanne Stiver (1983) 'Immigrant Women and their Work: A Study of British, Yugoslavian and Chilean Immigrant Women in Norway', *Scandinavian Journal of Development Alternatives*, Vol. 2, No. 3, Stockholm: Bethany Books.

Lynch, James F. (1989) *Border Khmer: A Democratic Study of the Residents of Site 2, Site B, and Site 8*, Bangkok: Ford Foundation.

Manz, Beatrice (1987) *Refugees of a Hidden War: The Aftermath of Counterinsurgency in Guatemala*, New York: State University of New York Press.

Miserez, Diana (ed.) (1988) *Refugees: The Trauma of Exile*, Dordrecht; Martinius Nijhoff Publishers.

Northwest Regional Educational Laboratory (1982–84) 'A Study of English Language Training for Refugees in the United States, Vols 1–111', Portland Oregon: Northwest Regional Educational Laboratory.

Overhagen, Mei Ying Van (1990) 'Refugee Women and International Relief Programs', in *Refugees in the World: The European Community's Response*, Utricht: Sim Special Issue 10.

Pittaway, Eileen (1990) 'We Want Help, Not Charity: Refugee Women in Australia Speak About Their Own Resettlement Needs', prepared for meeting of the UN Division for the Advancement of Women (Doc. No. EGM/RDWC/1990/CS. 1-2, July 1990).

Ramallah's Pioneer Mothers (1990) *Palestine Refugees Today*, No. 127.

Refugee Policy Group (nd) *Refugees Concern All of Us*, Washington, DC.

———— (1988) *New Branches . . . Distant Roots*, Washington, DC.

Refugee Women in Development (1988) *The Quilting Bee*, Potomac and Washington, DC: Texpress Publishing Group.

Reynell, Josephine (1989) *Political Pawns*, Oxford: Refugee Studies Programme.

Roulet-Billard, Annick (1989) 'First Person Feminine', *Refugees*, Vol. 70.

Sadosky, Cora (1988) 'Causes of Emigration of Scientists from Latin America', in *Scientists in Exile*, Washington, DC American Association for the Advancement of Science.

Sheehy, Gail and Mohn (1989) 'Who Will Help the Children of Nowhere?', *Parade*, 27 August.

Spencer-Simmons, Noreen (1990) 'Refugee Women at Risk: A Canadian Case Study', paper prepared for a meeting of the UN Division for the Advancement of Women (DOC. No.EGM/RDWC/1990/CS. 4-2, July 1990).

Snyder, Margaret (1990) *Women: The Key to Ending Hunger*, New York: The Hunger Project.

Spero, Abby (1985) *In America and In Need: Immigrant, Refugee and Entrant Women*, Washington, DC: American Association of Community and Junior Colleges and the US Department of Labor Women's Bureau.

Tenhula, John (1991) *Voices from Southeast*

Asia, New York: Holmes and Meier.

UN Commission on Human Rights (1991) UNESC E/CN.4/1991/L.34, *Resolution on Internally Displaced Persons*, New York: United Nations.

UN Department of Economic and Social Affairs (1975) *Popular Participation in Decision Making for Development*, New York: United Nations.

UN Economic and Social Council (1990) Resolution 1990/78, 'Refugees, Displaced Persons and Returnees', New York: United Nations.

UN General Assembly (1980) Resolution 35/135, 'Refugee and Displaced Women', New York: United Nations.

UN High Commissioner for Refugees (1991), 'A Framework for People-Oriented Planning in Refugee Situations', Geneva: UNHCR.

———— (1990a) *Assessment of Global Resettlement Needs and Priorities for Refugees in 1991*, Geneva: UNHCR.

———— (1990b) 'Food Deficits and Nutritional Consequences in Ten Selected Refugee Populations', prepared for a meeting with NGOs.

———— (1990c) 'Guinea: An Assessment of the Situation of Liberian Refugee Women and Children', Geneva: UNHCR.

———— (1982) *Handbook for Emergencies – Part One: Field Operations*, Geneva: UNHCR.

———— (1990d) 'Mission Report, Hong Kong: A Review of the Situation of Refugee Women and Children', Geneva: UNHCR.

———— (1990e) 'Note on Refugee Women and International Protection', Geneva: UNHCR.

———— (1990f), 'Policy on Refugee Women', Geneva: UNHCR.

———— (1990g) 'Report of the Permanent Working Group on the Situation of Women in UNHCR'. Geneva: UNHCR.

———— (1989) *Refugee Women: A Selected and Annotated Bibliography* (revised and updated), Geneva: UNHCR Centre for Documentation on Refugees.

———— (1983) 'Refugee Aid and Development', Executive Committee, Thirty-fourth Session (AIAC, 96/627) 12 September 1983 (contains report of the meeting of experts).

———— (1985) 'UNHCR and Refugee Women: International Protection', Geneva: UNHCR.

UNICEF (1986) *Assisting in Emergencies: A Resource Handbook for UNICEF Field Staff*, New York: UNICEF.

———— Office of the Special Representative in Phnom Penh (1990) *Cambodia: The Situation of Children and Women*, Phnom Penh: UNICEF.

Vena Newsletter (1990) 'Refugee and Displaced Women', Vol. 2, No. 2., Leiden, The Netherlands: Research and Documentation Centre on Women and Autonomy.

Weiss-Fagen, Patricia and Arturo Caballero-Barron (1987) 'Refugee Participation Case Study: Guatemalans in Campeche and Quintana Roo, Mexico', Washington, DC: Refugee Policy Group.

Williams, Tessa and Jeff Crisp (1989) 'Namibia Together Again', *Refugees*, Vol. 79.

Wingo, Gunillio (1990), 'Female Attitudes and Social Well-Being: Preparing Repatriation, A Pilot Study in Two Afghan Refugee Villages in Baluchistan', Quetta: UNHCR and Radd Barnen/Swedish Save the Children.

Women's Commission for Refugee Women and Children (1990), 'Report of Delegation to Hong Kong, January 5-12 1990', New York: International Rescue Committee.

World YWCA (1989) Papers, 'International Women in Namibia'. Geneva.

An extensive bibliography on refugee women can be found in (1989) *Refugee Women: A Selected and Annotated Bibliography* (revised and updated), Geneva: UNHCR Centre for

Documentation on Refugees. The
bibliography can be ordered from UNHCR,
Case postale 2500, 1211 Genève 2 Dépôt.

A complete set of papers prepared for the
Experts Meeting on Refugee and Displaced
Women, convened by the UN Division on
the Status of Women, can be ordered from:
The Division for the Advancement of
Women, United Nations Office Vienna, PO
Box 500, A-1400 Vienna, Austria.

AUDIO-VISUAL MATERIALS

Sigaalow, Town of Dust (1980, colour, 20
minutes; English/French/German)
A day in the life of a woman and her family
in a refugee camp in Somalia.
Women Refugees (1980, colour, 32 minutes;
English/French/German/Italian)
The special plight of refugee women and girls.

Ave Maria (1986, colour, 24 minutes;
English/French/German)
Compiled from footage filmed in Africa,
Asia, Central America and Europe, this
documentary shows the precarious
existence of refugee women and children.
Partners in Solutions (1990, colour, 8
minutes; English, video only)
An overview, for training purposes, of
protection and assistance measures for
refugee women.

For a wide selection of publications on
women's issues in general:

Zed Books Ltd	Zed Books Ltd
57 Caledonian Road	165 First Avenue
London N1 9BU	Atlantic Highlands
UK	New Jersey 07716
	USA

INDEX